THE EARTH WILL
BE FILLED
A Biblical Theology of
the Glory of God

DONNIE BERRY

ivp
Academic
An imprint of InterVarsity Press
Downers Grove, Illinois

InterVarsity Press
P.O. Box 1400 | Downers Grove, IL 60515-1426
ivpress.com | email@ivpress.com

InterVarsity Press® is the publishing division of InterVarsity Christian Fellowship/USA®. For more information, visit intervarsity.org.

Scripture quotations, unless otherwise noted, are from The Holy Bible, English Standard Version. ESV© Text Edition: 2016. Copyright © 2001 by Crossway Bibles, a publishing ministry of Good News Publishers. Used by permission. All rights reserved.

The publisher cannot verify the accuracy or functionality of website URLs used in this book beyond the date of publication.

Cover design: Faceout Studio, Addie Lutzo
Interior design: Daniel van Loon
Image: © Aaish grafico via Shutterstock

ISBN 978-1-5140-1077-8 (print) | ISBN 978-1-5140-1078-5 (digital)

Printed in the United States of America ∞

Library of Congress Cataloging-in-Publication Data
Names: Berry, Donald L. author
Title: The Earth will be filled : a biblical theology of the glory of God /
   Donnie Berry.
Description: Downers Grove, IL : IVP Academic, [2025] | Series: Essential
   studies of biblical theology series | Includes bibliographical
   references and index.
Identifiers: LCCN 2025021055 (print) | LCCN 2025021056 (ebook) | ISBN
   9781514010778 paperback | ISBN 9781514010785 ebook
Subjects: LCSH: Bible–Theology | Glory of God–Biblical teaching | Glory
   of God–Christianity
Classification: LCC BS543 .B47 2025 (print) | LCC BS543 (ebook) | DDC
   231/.4–dc23/eng/20250728
LC record available at https://lccn.loc.gov/2025021055
LC ebook record available at https://lccn.loc.gov/2025021056

32 31 30 29 28 27 26 25 | 13 12 11 10 9 8 7 6 5 4 3 2 1

"The glory of God is beautiful and lovely. It is the reason God created the world and the purpose of our lives. Donnie Berry aptly summarizes this central theme by conducting a tour of the biblical story line. Readers will be encouraged, strengthened, and full of praise as they reflect on God's splendor."

Thomas R. Schreiner, James Buchanan Harrison Professor of New Testament Interpretation at the Southern Baptist Theological Seminary

"This insightful study shows the centrality—and beauty—of God's glory across the whole of Scripture. It also invites readers to discern that glory in their lives and across the entire span of human history and enterprise. Talk of God's glory is common; deep analysis of its substance, contours, and effects is harder to come by. This book fills an acute need with admirable succinctness and real-life applications."

Robert W. Yarbrough, professor of New Testament at Covenant Theological Seminary

For Clay,

my first Romans teacher,

my first Greek teacher,

and a friend and brother who has loved at all times

and always stood beside me in adversity (Prov 17:17).

CONTENTS

SERIES PREFACE

L. MICHAEL MORALES

BIBLICAL THEOLOGY HAS SURELY entered a spring season, causing all who love the Scriptures to rejoice in the beauty and strength of its array of blossoms. Happily, since the original Essential Studies in Biblical Theology has proven to be a particularly ripe vine, IVP Academic has extended its publication for another round of volumes in the series, in good hope of further fruit.

From the dozens of dissertations coming out of biblical studies departments, and technical monographs of established scholars, down to weekly ministry-related blogposts, the increasing output of works of biblical theology has continued unabated. Nevertheless, the special features of the ESBT series, which led to its popularity, remain unique and ensure its vital place and contribution. ESBT has found that superb and extremely difficult balance of canon-wide exegesis and a warm, lay-level tone—solid scholarship for the church's delight.

For this second round of ESBT volumes, therefore, readers can expect an offering of major themes, purveyed in the full sweep of redemptive history, from Eden (Gen 1–3) to the new Jerusalem (Rev 21–22). Once more, sound scholarship will be wed to accessibility, both in terms of writing style and the relatively brief length of each volume. With skillful attention to nuanced development, authors will unfold their subjects in relation to the advent of the Messiah, the person and work of the Lord Jesus, and with an eye to practical application for the people of God in today's world. Our sincere hope and prayer is that these further volumes will encourage every reader not only to grasp the story and message of the Scriptures more deeply, finding his or her own place within its story, but to know, love, and adore the triune God of the Bible, and so to serve him with greater joy and gladness.

THE BEDROCK OF GLORY

THIS IS A "WHY?" SORT OF BOOK. Most toddlers go through the infamous "Why?" phase. No matter what you say, no matter what the situation, they want to know, "Why?" You give them an answer, and again they ask, "Why?" The cycle goes on and on forever, until you finally get down to some sort of bedrock at the bottom that mercifully liberates you from the interrogation. Usually it's something like, "Because I said so, that's why!" Or, in your more spiritual moments, "That's just the way God made it." Case closed. Bedrock.

At some point in my adult life I reentered the "Why?" phase. I want to trace everything back to bedrock, to its ultimate foundation. Like joy, for example. It's the thing we're all after. But where does joy come from? Why is it such a big deal to us? Why do we so desperately long for it? And when we long for joy, what is it we are really, at bottom, longing for?

Or another example: work. It comprises such a big part of our daily lives. But why do we work? Is it mainly a means to get a paycheck in order to finance the nonwork parts of our lives? Or is there a bigger purpose in our work? Why do we long for our work to be meaningful? And what gives it that meaning?

On and on it goes, attempting to trace everything back to its origin, to the why behind it all.

Here's what I've found: the bedrock—for joy and for work and for all things good and beautiful and true—is the same. It's the glory of God. The glory of Father, Son, and Holy Spirit.

GOD'S GLORY AS BEDROCK IN THE BIBLE

Everywhere I have dug in the Bible, I have hit the same bedrock. Whether Moses, the psalmists, the prophets, Jesus himself in the Gospels, or the apostles in the letters of the New Testament, all have led me back to the beautiful bedrock of "the light of the knowledge of the glory of God in the face of Jesus Christ" (2 Cor 4:6).

God's glory was Jesus' aim during his earthly ministry. It is what he came from heaven to reveal: "The Word became flesh and dwelt among us, and we have seen his glory, glory as of the only Son from the Father, full of grace and truth" (Jn 1:14). It is also the ultimate purpose for which Jesus went to the cross, as the opening words to his high priestly prayer express: "Father, the hour has come; glorify your Son that the Son may glorify you" (Jn 17:1). The "hour" in John's Gospel refers to the Son's death on the cross. In going to the cross, Jesus had his Father's glory in view: "Now is my soul troubled. And what shall I say? 'Father, save me from this hour'? But for this purpose I have come to this hour. Father, glorify your name" (Jn 12:27-28).

God's glory is also the aim Paul calls believers to pursue in everything they do: "So, whether you eat or drink, or whatever you do, do all to the glory of God" (1 Cor 10:31). Similarly, Peter exhorts believers to serve one another with their gifts in such a way that "in everything God may be glorified through Jesus Christ. To him belong glory and dominion forever and ever. Amen" (1 Pet 4:11).

God's glory was Jesus' aim. God's glory is to be our aim. And this is because, as the Bible shows, God's glory is his own aim.

- God *creates* for his glory: "everyone who is called by my name, whom I created for my glory" (Is 43:7).
- God *withholds anger* and *extends mercy* for his glory: "For my own sake, for my own sake, I do it, for how should my name be profaned? My glory I will not give to another" (Is 48:11).

- God *exalts Jesus* for his glory: "Therefore God has highly exalted him and bestowed on him the name that is above every name, so that at the name of Jesus every knee should bow, in heaven and on earth and under the earth, and every tongue confess that Jesus Christ is Lord, to the glory of God the Father" (Phil 2:9-11).
- God *blesses us in Christ with every spiritual blessing* for his glory: He chooses, predestines, adopts, redeems, forgives, lavishes with grace, and seals his people with the promised Holy Spirit, all "to the praise of his glory" (Eph 1:14).

The psalmist rejoices that God has "set [his] glory above the heavens" (Ps 8:1). And God's above-the-heavens glory will also fill the earth: "For the earth will be filled with the knowledge of the glory of the LORD as the waters cover the sea" (Hab 2:14).

In the grand, sweeping narrative of the Bible, the end of all things for all eternity is the glory of God, as many of the doxologies of the New Testament proclaim:

For from him and through him and to him are all things. *To him be glory forever.* Amen. (Rom 11:36)

To the only wise God be glory forevermore through Jesus Christ! Amen. (Rom 16:27)

To him be glory in the church and in Christ Jesus throughout all generations, forever and ever. Amen. (Eph 3:21)

To our God and Father be glory forever and ever. Amen. (Phil 4:20)

To the King of the ages, immortal, invisible, the only God, *be honor and glory* forever and ever. Amen. (1 Tim 1:17)

To him who loves us and has freed us from our sins by his blood and made us a kingdom, priests to his God and Father, *to him be glory* and dominion forever and ever. Amen. (Rev 1:5-6)

Again and again, in myriad ways, the Scriptures point to the aim toward which all Christian praise is directed and all of God's acts in creation and redemption are oriented: "Glory to God in the highest!" (Lk 2:14).

Of course, prooftexts such as these only show so much. To really see the richness of the theme of the glory of God in the Bible, we have to enter the Bible's story. As we do, we will see how God's glory gives shape to his unified purpose that runs through redemptive history, from creation all the way through to new creation. I hope you will come away in awe of the glory of God that stands at the heart of the gospel and the story of the Bible, of who God is, what he has done, and why he has done it. It all comes back to glory. This is bedrock. Wonderful bedrock.

But it raises a couple of questions that will be helpful to address up front before we strike out and trace this bedrock theme through the unfolding narrative of Scripture. First, what do we mean by glory, and specifically the glory of God? And second, what about God's love? Does all this emphasis on God seeking his own glory run counter to the revelation of his others-oriented, self-giving love in the Bible? Let me address these questions in turn.

WHAT IS GLORY?

Certain words and concepts resist easy definition. *Glory*, particularly as the Bible uses it with reference to God, is one of them.[1]

In a general sense, *glory* refers to the praise, honor, or esteem that results when a person accomplishes something great or is impressive in some way. Historically, kings and generals gained glory through winning battles, conquering lands, and accumulating extravagant wealth. Today, athletes and sports teams chase glory through winning championships or going for gold in the Olympics.

But what about the glory of God? We sing about God's glory in our worship songs. We pray for God to be glorified in situations we are facing. And we know in a vague, fuzzy way what we mean. Part of the aim of this study, though, is to push past vague notions of glory into a crisper (and more storied) understanding of what the Bible means when it speaks of the glory of God or calls us to glorify him.

So, let's begin with two important words. First, the Hebrew word *kābôd*, commonly translated "glory" in our English versions of the Old Testament.

---

[1]For some ways individuals over the last few centuries have attempted to define God's glory, see "Appendix B: 'The Glory of God' Defined by Various Theologians."

In a descriptive scene in 1 Samuel, we are told, "Eli fell over backward from his seat by the side of the gate, and his neck was broken and he died, for the man was old and *heavy*" (*kābôd*; 1 Sam 4:18). Translation: Eli was overweight—a man of great "heaviness" or "weightiness." That's *kābôd* in its most basic sense. It refers to something or someone that is heavy or weighty.

By extension, *kābôd* characterizes a person of great importance, worthy of honor and respect—a person of weight or glory. This could be the result of a person's abundant wealth, or the weight of their achievements, or because of standout qualities of character. For example, Joseph, who was exalted to second in command over Egypt, asked his brothers to go and "tell my father of all my *glory* [*kābôd*] in Egypt" (Gen 45:13). Joseph had become a weighty person.

That's *kābôd*: weightiness, honor, glory.

Now for the second important word: *doxa*, a Greek word commonly translated "glory" in English versions of the Bible. You may recognize this word from our English *doxology*, which is an ascription of praise to God, and also the title of the well-known hymn: "Praise God from whom all blessings flow." When the Hebrew Bible was first translated into Greek during the third and second centuries BC, *doxa* was the word the translators most commonly used to translate the Hebrew *kābôd*. Thus *doxa*, which in usage outside the Bible simply meant "opinion" or "reputation," came to assume the basic meanings and connotations of *kābôd*.

This shaped how the New Testament authors use *doxa*. As with *kābôd* in the Old Testament, *doxa* in the New Testament is frequently associated with honor or esteem (a high opinion or reputation), and to "glorify" someone is to give honor or praise to them. Jesus, for example, told a parable about taking the lowest seat at a banquet, so that when the host comes, he might say, "'Friend, move up higher.' Then you will be *glorified* [*doxazō*, the verbal form of *doxa*] in the presence of all who sit at table with you" (Lk 14:10 ESV altered). Similarly, Jesus criticizes the religious leaders for seeking the glory (*doxa*) that comes from one another rather than that which comes from God (Jn 5:44). *Glory*, in these instances, refers to honor given or sought.

But the real theological richness of these words—and the larger concept they provide a window into—comes as a result of the way the biblical authors use them with reference to God. The psalmist, for example, calls people to "ascribe to the LORD glory [*kābôd*] and strength. Ascribe to the LORD the glory [*kābôd*] due his name" (Ps 29:1-2). There are two instances of *glory* here, each with a slightly different shade of meaning. In the first instance, glory is an attribute of God, set alongside strength. The psalmist wants believers to acknowledge the worth or weightiness of God—who God is, what he is like. This is his glory. In the second instance, people are to respond to God's glory by "ascrib[ing] to the LORD the glory due his name." Here *glory* refers to the honor God deserves as a result of who he is. Because of his glory, he is to be glorified.

In its theological sense, *glory* is first and foremost a descriptor for God. It is something of a summary term the Bible uses to describe God's character and nature, his attributes and his essence. It's all the things God is in himself that make him worthy of honor and praise. In the book of Exodus, for example, Moses asks God, "Please show me your glory" (Ex 33:18). The Lord responds by saying, "I will make all my goodness pass before you and will proclaim before you my name" (Ex 33:19). The Lord then hides Moses in a cleft of a rock and passes before him, proclaiming the name, character, and attributes of God: "The LORD, the LORD, a God merciful and gracious, slow to anger and abounding in steadfast love and faithfulness" (Ex 34:6). God shows Moses who he is and what he is like. He shows him his glory.

Especially important are the ways the biblical authors use the phrase "the glory of the Lord" (or "the glory of God"), which occurs frequently in both the Old and New Testaments.

The glory [*kābôd*] of the Lord dwelt on Mount Sinai. . . . Now the appearance of the glory [*kābôd*] of the LORD was like a devouring fire on the top of the mountain in the sight of the people of Israel. (Ex 24:16-17)

The glory [*kābôd*] of the LORD filled the tabernacle. (Ex 40:34)

And the glory [*kābôd*] of the LORD shall be revealed, and all flesh shall see it together. (Is 40:5)

In these examples from the Old Testament, God's glory appears as something concrete, visible, seen, and experienced. It dwells on Sinai, fills the tabernacle, and will be revealed to all humanity. The following examples from the New Testament are similar:

> An angel of the Lord appeared to them, and the glory [*doxa*] of the Lord shone around them. (Lk 2:9)

> And we all, with unveiled face, beholding the glory [*doxa*] of the Lord, are being transformed into the same image, from one degree of glory [*doxa*] to another. (2 Cor 3:18)

> He is the radiance of the glory [*doxa*] of God and the exact imprint of his nature. (Heb 1:3)

Again, in these passages God's glory takes a definite shape. It is seeable or knowable in an experiential way. The Scriptures bear witness to (1) God's internal glory—his very character and nature, (2) externally revealed and put on display, (3) so that his glory might be seen, acknowledged, and responded to in ways appropriate to such glory. This is what we find in the examples above: God's glory made manifest, sometimes in physical form, which is representative of who God is in his magnificent greatness.

Glory is God's very nature. Glory is the revelation of his nature. And glory is the honor given him in response to the revelation of his nature. This is how the Bible speaks of God's glory.

Bringing all this together, here is how I might attempt to define *glory* as the Bible uses it in its rich, theological sense: *Glory refers to all the fullness of the triune God—the fullness of his wisdom, love, creativity, beauty, strength, compassion, justice, life, joy—all that makes him weighty and wonderful, made manifest for us to see, experience, respond to, and, perhaps most surprisingly, participate in.*

This is capital-*G* glory. There are many little-*g* glories in the Bible. The glory of kings. The glory of nations. The glory of specific individuals. But there is only one capital-*G* Glory. God's Glory. The original and ultimate Glory. This is the bedrock beneath the Bible's story, the solid foundation on which everything else is built.

GOD'S GLORY OR HIS LOVE?

But what about God's love? Early in my doctoral studies, one of my professors shared his difficulty with the idea that God creates or redeems for his own glory. For him, this seemed to run counter to God's others-oriented love and grace that are so central in the Bible. He felt that for God to act in order to glorify himself suggests that God is somehow deficient and in need of glorification, which he knew didn't square with the picture of God revealed in Scripture.

This is a valid concern. We don't tend to admire individuals whose main pursuit is their personal glory. We admire those who put the good of others above their own position or praise. So why would we admire God for pursuing his own glory? Why doesn't this make him "a self-centered, self-referential being, whose basic motivation for what he does, including his motivation for saving people, is so that he might receive more glory," as one biblical scholar contends?[2] The reason has everything to do with what God's glory is and what it means for him to pursue his glory.

God is not deficient in glory, as though his pursuit of glory were intended to fill up some lack in himself. He is a God of fullness, an overflowing fountain, as theologians have often described him. In God is fullness of love, fullness of strength, fullness of life, and fullness of joy. This is his glory. In love, he shares his glory with us so that we might share in his fullness and joy.

God's pleasure in doing this, says theologian Jonathan Edwards, "is rather a pleasure in diffusing and *communicating* to, than in *receiving* from, the creature. Surely, it is no argument of indigence in God that he is inclined to communicate of his infinite fullness. It is no argument of the emptiness or deficiency of a fountain, that it is inclined to overflow."[3]

All that is truly good, delightful, and beautiful has its origins in the glory of God. God does all he does so that his glory might be seen and enjoyed and shared with his people for their ultimate good and for their joy and delight. This is what it means for God to pursue his glory. He does this because he *is* love.

For humans, the choice to pursue our own glory often stands in tension with the choice to love others. For God, this is not the case. He magnifies

---

[2]Ben Witherington, "'For God So Loved Himself?' Is God a Narcissist?," Beliefnet, November 20, 2007, www.beliefnet.com/columnists/bibleandculture/2007/11/for-god-so-loved-himself-is-god -a-narcissist.html.

[3]Jonathan Edwards, *The End for Which God Created the World*, in John Piper, *God's Passion for His Glory: Living the Vision of Jonathan Edwards, with the Complete Text of The End for Which God Created the World* (Wheaton, IL: Crossway, 1998), 165.

what is of ultimate value and worth—his glory—and shares it with his people for their good and for their eternal joy. It is the greatest way the God of glory loves his people.

In the coming chapters, as we follow the theme of God's glory through the story of the Bible, we will see how wonderfully inseparable God's pursuit of his glory and his love for his people are. We will find that God's commitment to his glory and his sacrificial, self-giving love are not at odds in the least. Rather, they are beautifully intertwined.

AN INVITATION TO JOY

In 1647, a group of English and Scottish Reformers penned the Westminster Catechism, with its now famous opening lines:

> Q. 1. *What is the chief end of man?*

> A. Man's chief end is to glorify God, and to enjoy him forever.

C. S. Lewis knew the catechism and thought deeply about these words. Reflecting on the common exhortation in the Psalms to glorify God or give praise to him, he made these insightful observations:

> It is frustrating to have discovered a new author and not to be able to tell anyone how good he is; to come suddenly, at the turn of the road, upon some mountain valley of unexpected grandeur and then to have to keep silent because the people with you care for it no more than for a tin can in the ditch; to hear a good joke and find no one to share it with. . . .
>
> If it were possible for a created soul fully . . . to "appreciate," that is to love and delight in, the worthiest object of all, and simultaneously at every moment to give this delight perfect expression, then that soul would be in supreme beatitude. . . . The Scotch catechism says that man's chief end is "to glorify God and enjoy Him forever." But we shall then know that these are the same thing. Fully to enjoy is to glorify. In commanding us to glorify Him, God is inviting us to enjoy Him.[4]

This is the invitation the God of glory, in his love, makes to us.

---

[4]C. S. Lewis, *Reflections on the Psalms* (New York: Harcourt, Brace and World, 1958), 95-97.

GOD'S GLORY AS THE BEDROCK OF JOY

My quest for bedrock has led me on a journey for answers to questions like the ones I raised previously: Where does joy come from? Why is it such a big deal to us? Why do we so desperately long for it? And when we long for joy, what is it we are really, at bottom, longing for? Lewis, the Westminster catechists, and the Bible give a clear and unmistakable answer: the glory of God.

Joy is born in the heart of God, who is intrinsically glorious and supremely weighty. We long for joy because we were made for God, and joy is the natural and appropriate response to knowing him and beholding his glory. When we long for joy, we are longing for God. We are longing to see his glory and to be drawn into it. We are longing to be captivated by his glory and to give expression to it. This is bedrock. This is what the story of the Bible is all about.

"Fully to enjoy is to glorify," Lewis says. "In commanding us to glorify Him, God is inviting us to enjoy Him." That is the invitation of this book. It's an invitation into the story of the Bible, which at its heart is about God's glory and our joy in him. It's an invitation to dig deep into the Scriptures and to discover there the solid bedrock of the glory of God.

Chapter One

GOD'S GLORY SHARED IN CREATION

*For the earth will be filled with the knowledge of
the glory of the Lord as the waters cover the sea.*

HABAKKUK 2:14

FOR OVER A DECADE, I taught the Old Testament to eighth graders
at a Christian school. Barely teenagers, the students were in many ways just
beginning to formulate their ideas about God and the world. Each fall, we
would begin our journey through the Old Testament in Genesis 1:1, "In the
beginning, God created the heavens and the earth." And each fall, I would
ask my new class of young theologians the same question, "Why?" Most of
the students had been taught from the time they were young that God is the
Creator of all that exists. Now I wanted them to think about *why* he created.

Without fail, year after year, the students would give the same answers:
"Because he was lonely." Or sometimes, "Because he was bored." This seemed
obvious to them. They knew that before he created the world, there was only
God. No one and nothing else existed. All that exists comes from God and
was created by God and for God. Students also knew that God created humans
in order to have a relationship with them.

But then they made a fatal assumption. If God existed "all by himself," he must have been lonely, or worse, bored. To an eighth grader, nothing could be more terrible. It made sense to them that God must have created the world so he would have something to do, and he created humans so he wouldn't be lonely.

At this point, I would enthusiastically exclaim, "No! Wrong answer!" Then I would explain why. I taught them about God's fullness and how there is no lack in him. I taught them about the Trinity, mysterious as it is, and how Father, Son, and Holy Spirit were not alone and bored as the students imagined, but enjoyed wonderful fellowship, eternally delighting in the inward perfections of God. I gave them an alternative "why" to correct their misguided instincts: *God created for his glory.*

TRIUNE GLORY

When the Scriptures give us a peek behind the curtains of creation into eternity, we find glory. Jesus prays, "Father, glorify me . . . with the glory that I had with you *before the world existed*" (Jn 17:5). The "Father of glory" (Eph 1:17) has eternally shared his glory with his Son, who is "the radiance of the glory of God and the exact imprint of his nature" (Heb 1:3). The Father expresses his love for his Son by giving his glory to him: "Father, I desire that they also, whom you have given me, may be with me where I am, to see *my glory that you have given me because you loved me before the foundation of the world*" (Jn 17:24).

Before creation, there was a perfect sharing of life, love, and glory between Father, Son, and Holy Spirit. This is the source and substance of the joy that eternally characterizes God's inner life. It is also the antidote to our impoverished imaginations that think of God's existence before creation as boring and lonely rather than breathtakingly beautiful and full. Fred Sanders, a well-known scholar and author on the Trinity, is instructive here:

> This inner life that God lives, in the happy land of the Trinity above all worlds, is a livelier life than any other life. . . . The knowledge that God enjoys perfect blessedness is a great thing. Even if it stays a kind of secret at the back of our minds, as something that we cannot say much about, it nevertheless exerts a tremendous gravitational pull on the rest of our thoughts and affections.[1]

---

[1]Fred Sanders, *The Deep Things of God: How the Trinity Changes Everything*, 2nd ed. (Wheaton, IL: Crossway, 2017), 86-87.

Life within God—in which Father, Son, and Spirit give, receive, and radiate God's glory—is a "lively life" full of joy and delight. It is a life of self-giving love—Father to Son and Son to Father through the Holy Spirit. This is the bedrock beneath the Bible's story and the air from which creation is breathed into existence.

The mysterious and wonderful relations within the Trinity do not come to full light in the story line of Scripture until the Son's incarnation. But it is important to mark from the outset that behind creation stands Father, Son, and Spirit in the fullness of glory. As Sanders asserts, "That life is so full that everything else comes from it, as a small trickle from an infinite plenty."[2]

"GOD CREATED FOR HIS GLORY"

Year after year I sought to create categories and conceptions in teenage minds for this fullness of glory that characterizes life in God. His glory, I explained, is all that he is—goodness, love, strength, wisdom, beauty, creativity, joy—all the things that make him infinitely better than every other thing we could imagine or desire. Sometimes I would attempt to adopt the lingua franca of my eighth graders, simply defining glory as "God's awesomeness on public display." I wanted my students to see that "the God of glory" (Ps 29:3; see Acts 1:7) stands as the fountainhead of creation, and creation flows out of "the riches of his glory" (Eph 3:16).

"God created for his glory," I would tell them. But that religious phrase is easy to affirm and at the same time have no real sense of its meaning, goodness, or gravity. So I aimed to fill it with meaning. Here's the basic idea I tried to communicate: *God, out of his infinite fullness, created the world to fill it with his glory. And he created humans to see his glory and to delight in it, to share in his glory and to display it. All this so that we and all creation might participate in God's eternal joy.*

This is the why of creation. These are weighty ideas, big for teenage minds, and for the rest of us too. I was never sure whether my students understood the difference between their answers and the one I was giving them, or whether it made sense to them why I was so insistent and passionate about it. But one

---

[2]Sanders, *Deep Things of God*, 87.

year, I knew at least one student got it. She raised her hand and said, "So, Mr. Berry, what you're saying is that God is the bomb. He knows he's the bomb. And he created the world to share his bomb diggity. Is that right?" Brilliantly right. Out of the mouths of infants and eighth graders (see Mt 21:16).

THE REVELATION OF GOD'S GLORY THROUGH CREATION

Nowhere in the creation account does the word *glory* occur. But biblical scholars and theologians have long recognized the error of equating words and concepts. The word *glory* does not occur in the early chapters of Genesis, but the *concept* runs rich and deep beneath all God's acts in Genesis 1–2.

When God creates, he does it by speaking: "And God said, 'Let there be light,' and there was light" (Gen 1:3). There are ten "And God said" moments in Genesis 1 (Gen 1:3, 6, 9, 11, 14, 20, 24, 26, 28-29). On the first page of the Bible we learn a simple but profound truth. God is a speaking God. He creates through his word:

> By the word of the LORD the heavens were made,
>> and by the breath of his mouth all their host. . . .
> For he spoke, and it came to be;
>> he commanded, and it stood firm. (Ps 33:6, 9)

In the Bible, God's word is a means by which he reveals himself. When he creates through his word, it is an act of divine self-expression. The apostle John, reflecting on this "In the beginning" act of creation (Jn 1:1), tells us that God's "word" by which he created the world is a personal word, his own eternal Son, the very one who reveals God's glory (Jn 1:14) and makes God known (Jn 1:18). In Genesis 1, when God creates through his word, he reveals himself. In creation, he communicates his glory.

The psalmist says of God's creation,

> The heavens declare the glory of God,
>> and the sky above proclaims his handiwork.
> Day to day pours out speech,
>> and night to night reveals knowledge. . . .
> Their voice goes out through all the earth,
>> and their words to the end of the world. (Ps 19:1-2, 4)

God's creation, spoken into existence, now speaks of him. Creation carries something of God's word—his own self-expression—within it.

This, I think, is why people are so moved by sunsets, mountains, starlit skies, and so many other aspects of creation. They are speaking to us of God's glory, giving expression to aspects of his character and nature—his greatness, his beauty, his creativity, his power, his wisdom, his generosity. There are echoes of God's voice within his creation. Even those who do not know or acknowledge God hear these echoes and are often stirred by them. Creation is like a canvas on which God has painted his glory. The created world is meant to lead us to know and worship and praise the Creator who is the source of this glory.

The apostle Paul understood this about creation. In his letter to the Romans, he says that "what can be known about God is plain to [all mankind], because God has shown it to them" (Rom 1:19). How, we might ask, has God shown it to them? Here is Paul's answer: "For his invisible attributes, namely, his eternal power and divine nature, have been clearly perceived ever since the creation of the world, *in the things that have been made*" (Rom 1:20). God's "invisible attributes" are known and perceived in the things he has created. That's what creation is for—to make the invisible attributes of God visible. Reformer John Calvin captures this idea, saying, "The world was no doubt made, that it might be the theatre of the divine glory."[3]

While *glory* does not verbally occur in the creation account, the concept is at the heart of creation. Through creation, God makes his character and nature known. He shares himself, "diffusing his own fullness," to borrow language from early American theologian Jonathan Edwards.[4] In Genesis 1 we first encounter glory in the Bible, as God speaks his divine word of self-revelation and self-expression, making aspects of his invisible glory visible in the things he has made. Creation bears the imprint of the glory of God.

---

[3]John Calvin, *Calvin's Commentaries* (Grand Rapids: Baker, 1979), 22:266.

[4]John Piper and Jonathan Edwards, *God's Passion for His Glory: Living the Vision of Jonathan Edwards, With the Complete Text of The End for Which God Created the World* (Wheaton, IL: Crossway, 1998), 165.

HUMANS AS GOD'S LIVING REPRESENTATIVES

It should come as no surprise, then, that human beings, the crown of God's creation, also carry the imprint of his glory. In fact, it is in the creation of humans that God's glory project in the world is set into full motion.

Genesis 1 tells us that God created humans as his own image, an idea that, in the biblical story, is closely linked with God's glory. Here's how the narrative reads:

> Then God said, "Let us make man in our image, after our likeness. And let them have dominion over the fish of the sea and over the birds of the heavens and over the livestock and over all the earth and over every creeping thing that creeps on the earth."

> So God created man in his own image,
>   in the image of God he created him;
>   male and female he created them. (Gen 1:26-27)

Of all that God makes, only humans are his image. This is the first thing we learn in the Bible about human beings, and it is foundational for understanding who we are and why we exist.

An image, in the Hebrew Bible, is a physical, three-dimensional representation of something else. For example, the Bible refers to idols as "images." Statues stood in temples throughout the ancient world to represent a deity, showing what that temple's god was like. Humans, though, are not inert statues depicting lifeless gods. God created humans to be living, breathing, physical representatives of the living God. He placed humans in the Garden of Eden, God's holy place, as his images who represent him in the world.

SONS AND DAUGHTERS OF GOD

The image of God was a familiar concept among the cultures surrounding Israel when Genesis was written. It communicated two interrelated ideas: sonship and kingship.[5] Pharaoh, for example, was considered the son of Ra (the Egyptian sun god), who ruled on Ra's behalf. As king, he was like a living statue—Ra's image—who represented Ra on earth. Both of these aspects—sonship and

---

[5]Peter J. Gentry and Stephen J. Wellum, *Kingdom Through Covenant: A Biblical-Theological Understanding of the Covenants*, 2nd ed. (Wheaton, IL: Crossway, 2018), 226-27.

kingship—are present in Genesis as well, though in a way that brings correction
to the notions held by pagan nations.

First, to be God's image means humans have a special relationship with God.
All human beings (and not just the king) are created to uniquely relate to God
as his sons and daughters. In Genesis 1:26, we overhear God's decree: "Let us
make man in our image, after our likeness." Just a few chapters later, we are told,
"Adam . . . fathered a *son* in his own likeness, after his image, and named him
Seth" (Gen 5:3). To be someone's image is connected to sonship. This is why
Luke, in tracing Jesus' lineage, refers to "Adam, *the son of God*" (Lk 3:38). When
the text of Genesis tells us that God created humans in his image, it is making
a *relational* claim—humans are related to God as Father just as Seth is related
to Adam as father. In creation, God makes humans his sons and daughters.

As sons and daughters, humans are able to uniquely know God and also
to uniquely represent him. The Father, in creation, brings them into his life,
glory, and love.

KINGS AND QUEENS OVER CREATION

This leads to a second aspect of being God's image, which is front and center
in the text of Genesis 1–2, a *vocational* aspect. God creates humans to rule
as his representatives and to spread his glory throughout creation: "Let us
make mankind in our image . . . *so that they may rule* over the fish in the sea
and the birds in the sky, over the livestock and all the wild animals, and over
all the creatures that move along the ground" (Gen 1:26 NIV).

Psalm 8 is David's ancient and inspired commentary on the creation
narrative in Genesis 1. David considers the role God gives to human beings
within creation. He acknowledges the apparent insignificance of mankind
as he surveys "the work of your fingers, the moon and the stars, which you
have set in place" (Ps 8:3). Given the majesty of God and of his creation, David
marvels, "What is man that you are mindful of him, and the son of man that
you care for him?" (Ps 8:4). He then makes this grand statement, rendering
in his own words the account given in Genesis 1:26:

> Yet you have made him a little lower than the heavenly beings
> and crowned him with glory and honor.

You have given him dominion over the works of your hands;
>   you have put all things under his feet,
all sheep and oxen,
>   and also the beasts of the field,
the birds of the heavens, and the fish of the sea,
>   whatever passes along the paths of the seas. (Ps 8:5-8)

When David reads Genesis 1:26, he sees the creation of humans in God's image as a bestowal of status, a crowning with glory and honor. This status, in both Genesis 1 and Psalm 8, is directly tied to their vocation. By creating humans as his image, God bestows on them incredible honor and a distinct vocation in his world. God crowns them with glory and gives them dominion over creation (Ps 8:5-8; see Gen 1:26, 28). Human glory is linked to their vocational status as rulers over God's world.

Significantly, by saying that God crowned humans with glory in what is a clear allusion to Genesis 1:26-28, David verbally links the concepts of image and glory together—an association that will only grow stronger in later Jewish writings, and especially in Paul's letters in the New Testament, where the two are often used almost interchangeably (see, e.g., Rom 8:29-30; 1 Cor 11:7; 2 Cor 3:18; 4:4). This connection between image and glory, and their close correlation to dominion over creation, takes us to the heart of the story that runs through the rest of the Bible.

God alone is king over his creation. Hezekiah declares God's kingship by virtue of his being the Creator of all things: "O LORD of hosts, God of Israel, *enthroned* above the cherubim, you are the God, you alone, of all the kingdoms of the earth; you have made heaven and earth" (Is 37:16).

Similarly, the psalmist exclaims:

For the LORD is a great God,
>   and *a great King* above all gods.
In his hand are the depths of the earth;
>   the heights of the mountains are his also.
The sea is his, for he made it,
>   and his hands formed the dry land. (Ps 95:3-5)

God created the world, and he is king over his world. Astonishingly, he chose humans—those uniquely related to him as sons and daughters—to exercise his good rule and reign in the world. God gives them a royal status. He crowns them with his glory (Ps 8:5) and appoints them his representative kings and queens over creation (Ps 8:6; Gen 1:26, 28). At creation, humans, who see and share in God's glory, are tasked with ruling as his images—caring for creation and spreading his glory throughout the earth.

Of course, we live in a world affected by the fall that occurs in Genesis 3 (the subject of the next chapter), and our experience is far different from the picture we see in Genesis 1–2. But we are still able to get a sense of the goodness God planned for his world (and the goodness he intends to restore to it) by going back to the beginning of the story at creation. What we find there is the kingdom of God on the very first page of Scripture—the good, life-giving, joy-bringing rule and reign of God to be exercised through those created in his image, who were to rule in his name and reflect his character, and whom he commissioned to carry his glory into every part of creation they would "fill" and "subdue" (Gen 1:28).

A KINGDOM SHAPED BY THE GLORY OF ITS KING

When I was younger and had ample free time, there were a handful of movies I watched over and over again. One of them was *First Knight*. It's a take on the legendary King Arthur and the kingdom of Camelot. In keeping with the legends, *First Knight* portrays Arthur as a good king, who has built Camelot around humility and service. His knights sit at the round table—a table of equals with no head—and their motto is, "In serving one another we become free."

Camelot is different from the oppressive, dark kingdoms that surround it. This is because Camelot's king is unlike other kings. Arthur champions justice, brotherhood, and sacrifice. He loves the people of his kingdom and is willing to give his life for them. The inhabitants of the kingdom follow their king and his ways, and so Camelot shines with goodness, beauty, and joy.

When, as a teenager, I watched *First Knight*, it struck a deep chord in me—a longing for a good king and for a different kind of kingdom. I now realize that, however imperfectly (and there are certainly complications in the plot), *First Knight* gave me a picture of what God purposed in creation. Arthur's kingdom reflects the kingdom of God.

God is a king unlike other kings—full of goodness, self-giving love, generosity, and joy. And his kingdom is meant to be shaped by its King, and by its citizens who are like their King and embody his character and heart in all they do, so that goodness, self-giving love, and joy fill the kingdom. This was God's design for his world and for his people. This is why he created.

To fulfill this vision, God's images must be like him. There is an *ethical* aspect to their glory. They are meant to embody holiness, righteousness, kindness, generosity, love, wisdom, humility, creativity, and so many other qualities of God's life, which God grants humans to participate in and display. Humans are not to exercise just any dominion but Godlike dominion—dominion that takes the form of self-giving love. In creation, God invests humans with his glory so they can participate in the joy of being like God, reflecting his self-giving love into every relationship, every task, and every part of creation he places under their care.

FRUITFUL AND FILLING THE EARTH

These facets of human glory—relational, vocational, and ethical—shine in the biblical story like light refracted from a diamond, filling with color the biblical theme of *God's glory revealed to and through humanity*. Sons and daughters of God, who are his representative rulers over creation, who reflect his character and nature into the world. Each of these facets is bound up with the creation mandate, which in the biblical text immediately follows the creation of humans as God's image: "And God blessed them. And God said to them, 'Be fruitful and multiply and fill the earth and subdue it, and have dominion over the fish of the sea and over the birds of the heavens and over every living thing that moves on the earth'" (Gen 1:28).

This blessing and mandate gives inaugural expression to the unified purpose of God that will run through creation, redemption, and new creation. All are the outworking of this commission, a partnership between God and humanity to fill the earth with the glory of God and to extend his good, wise, loving, and life-giving kingship to every corner of creation.

The creation mandate reverberates through the story of the Bible. God blesses humanity, an act by which he enables them to be and do all that he created them to be and do. Then he invests them with his divine purpose for his people.

First, they are to "be fruitful and multiply and fill the earth." This is not just a numerical project, aimed at populating the planet. It is about filling the planet *with his image*—humans who know God and see his glory, those who rule as God's image and so will fill the earth with his glory as they increase in number.

That's what the second part of the commission is about. Humans are to subdue the earth and have dominion over it, extending God's kingship through self-giving love that reflects his glory and brings the goodness, flourishing, and joy of his reign to everything, everywhere. When we seek the good of others and go low to lift others up, when we express loving care for creation and develop wise and just systems and structures that lead to order, abundance, and life, then we are giving expression to the glory of God.

God's intention was for his royal images to "expand the borders of Eden to the uttermost parts of the world."[6] Those who see and share in God's glory are now called to multiply and fill the earth with God's dominion, causing his glory, which they carry, to shape every facet of creation.

A WORLD FILLED WITH GLORY

The themes of Genesis 1:28 run through the rest of the book of Genesis and will shape the biblical story going forward. Especially noteworthy is the way the phrase "fill the earth" is appropriated and deployed by biblical authors. Specifically, there is a shared understanding that this statement from Genesis 1:28 is about the earth being *filled with God's glory*, an idea that becomes a promise and a prayer in later Scripture. In Numbers 14:21, God pledges that "all the earth shall be filled with the glory of the LORD." The psalmists repeat the chorus, "Be exalted, O God, above the heavens! Let your glory be over all the earth" (Ps 57:5, 11; 108:5). Similarly, Psalm 72—a psalm that portrays the worldwide rule and reign of the Messiah and also, significantly, ends the prayers of David contained in Books 1 and 2 of the Psalter—concludes with this doxology:

---

[6]Gentry and Wellum, *Kingdom Through Covenant*, 832.

Blessed be the LORD, the God of Israel,
    who alone does wondrous things.
Blessed be his glorious name forever;
    may the whole earth be filled with his glory!
Amen and Amen! (Ps 72:18-19)

In Isaiah's vision of the glory of the Lord, the seraphim cry in anticipation of what is to come: "The whole earth is full of his glory" (Is 6:3). And the prophet Habakkuk makes a grand declaration that sums up God's plan for creation: "For the earth will be filled with the knowledge of the glory of the LORD as the waters cover the sea" (Hab 2:14).

The refrain of God's glory filling the earth echoes through the pages of the Bible. It expresses God's purpose for humans, whom he created for a unique relationship with him and a privileged role within creation. From creation onward, God has intended to reveal his character to and through his sons and daughters. What God is by nature, he has determined to display on the canvas of creation. Human beings, made in the image of God, are the Artist's brush, designed to paint his glory across the globe.

SHARING IN AND SPREADING GOD'S ETERNAL GLORY

As we trace the theme of God's glory through Scripture, we will mark its development with the following diagram, which we will revisit at each stage in the story. This will provide us with a simple, visual depiction of the unified purpose of God that runs through redemptive history.

A. (See Figure 1.1) Everything flows from God's wonderful, eternal glory, shared between Father, Son, and Spirit (depicted here with the triquetra, a common symbol for the Trinity).

B. God creates the world as a place to be filled with his glory.

C. And God creates humans as the crown of his creation.

D. (See Figure 1.2) He creates humans for a unique relationship with himself, bringing them into the loving relationship eternally shared between Father, Son, and Spirit. God creates them in his image, to be sons and daughters, those whom he loves and with whom he shares his glory.

E. From this special relationship with God, humans are given a unique role within creation. They serve as kings and queens, glory sharers and glory

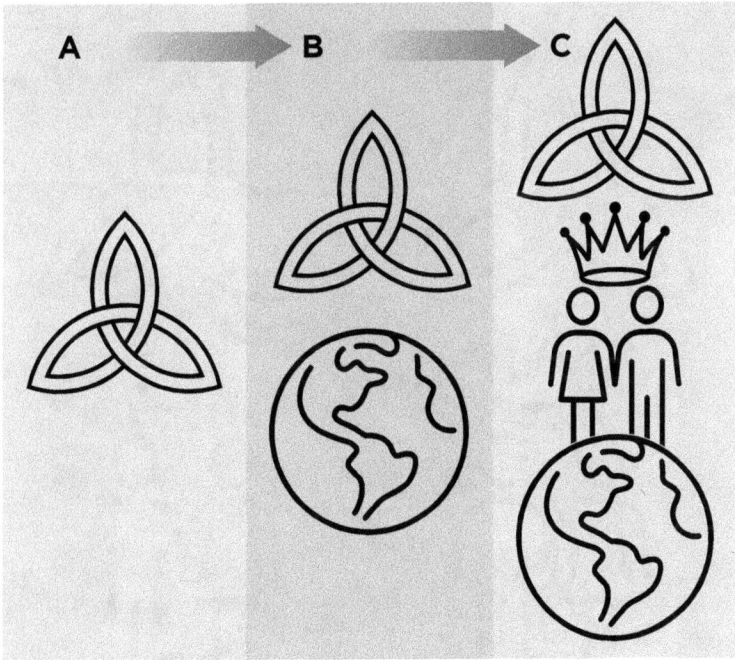

Figure 1.1. God creates to fill the earth with his glory

spreaders. They are to fill the earth and leave the imprint of God's glory on every part of his world, so that everything in creation drips with his glory, so to speak. In this way, the whole earth will be filled with the glory of the Lord—with the fullness of his life and love and joy—as the waters cover the sea (Hab 2:14).

BRINGING THE GOODNESS OF GOD'S DOMINION TO ALL CREATION

This is how the story of the Bible opens. It's a wonderful beginning, appropriately declared "very good" by the author. In fact, there are six "and God saw that it was good" statements in Genesis 1 (Gen 1:4, 10, 12, 18, 21, 25), which culminate in a seventh, exultant affirmation of creation's goodness: "And God saw everything that he had made, and behold, it was very good" (Gen 1:31).

God's creation was "very good" but not yet all that it would be. We can think of creation as an untamed wilderness, teeming with life and beauty but in need of care and cultivation to draw out that beauty and give shape to

Figure 1.2. God creates humans to share in and to spread his glory

its life. For example, at the beginning of the creation account in Genesis 2, the author says that "no small plant of the field had yet sprung up" because "there was no man to work the ground" (Gen 2:5). These "small plants of the field" refer specifically to cultivated grains.[7] The plants could not grow and

---

[7]Mark Futato, "Because It Had Rained: A Study of Genesis 2:5-7 with Implications for Genesis 2:4-25 and Genesis 1:1–2:3," *Westminster Theological Journal* 60, no. 1 (1998): 4-5.

produce grain without humans to work the ground and draw out the earth's fruitfulness. To meet this need, "the LORD God formed the man of dust from the ground" (Gen 2:7) and placed him in the Garden of Eden to work and keep it (Gen 2:8, 15).

We also learn that a river flowed out of Eden, branching into four smaller rivers: "The name of the first is the Pishon; it winds through the entire land of Havilah, where there is gold. (The gold of that land is good; aromatic resin and onyx are also there)" (Gen 2:11-12 NIV). These easy-to-overlook details in the text are not insignificant. They tell us that God has embedded within creation wonderful resources. Part of human dominion is discovering, cultivating, and turning the raw materials of creation into objects of usefulness and beauty. God authorizes his royal images to bring the goodness of his rule and reign to the rest of creation, drawing out all the creative potential embedded within God's world and causing the whole creation to flourish and reflect his glory. This looks like growing, caring for, and creating things— gardens, as we see in Genesis 2, but also families, communities, cities, governments, schools, technologies, businesses, art, music, poetry, culinary delights, and much, much more.

Creation was "very good," primed by God to become all he created it to be. He infused creation with aspects of his glory. Above all, he set his sons and daughters over his world, inviting them to work with him to make the world all he intends—each person reflecting aspects of God's character and nature, causing the things they touch to bear the imprint of the king, so that the whole kingdom would shine with God's glory and overflow with joy and praise.

Theologian Michael Reeves writes, "Indeed, in the triune God is the love behind all love, the life behind all life, the music behind all music, the beauty behind all beauty and the joy behind all joy."[8] The royal calling of God's people was to spread God's love, life, music, beauty, and joy, so that it would fill creation and direct the hearts of men and women back to the one who is the source of it all. In this way, all creation would be filled with God's presence

---

[8]Michael Reeves, *Delighting in the Trinity: An Introduction to the Christian Faith* (Downers Grove, IL: IVP Academic, 2012), 62.

and glory as his people multiplied and filled the earth with his good rule and reign.

WHY WE WORK

When we understand this, it wonderfully expands our sense of what it means to glorify God in our lives. I served as a college pastor for many years, working with students who spent the majority of their week in classes designed to help them prepare for careers. One of my aims was to help them see all of life in relationship to God and his grand story. But early on, I did not have a place for understanding how their careers fit into the big story of the Bible. Why do we work? How does our work fit into God's plan for his world? What does it mean to glorify God in our work? I mostly saw work as a way to earn money to support the work of the church or missions in the world. If there was anything distinctively Christian and God-glorifying in nine-to-five jobs, it was being moral in the workplace and evangelizing or inviting your co-workers to church. Those are good things, but I was missing a big piece of the story.

Alongside serving as a college pastor, I was doing doctoral studies, exploring biblical theology and especially the relationship between God's image and God's glory in the Bible. When I began to get a sense of God's plan for his world and of his design for humans to participate in his plan, it enlarged my sense of the goodness of our work. The work itself is part of God's plan to fill all creation with his glory. The sphere of work he gives us is a place we get to fill, subdue, and bring God's loving, life-giving kingship to bear. We get to bring order, creativity, love, and flourishing to the spheres of influence God entrusts to us. God shares his glory with us so that we might use our gifts in industries of service, art, education, business, technology, government, and countless others, bringing beauty and blessing to the world through the work of our hands.

The thing we spend the majority of our week doing is not just an aside to the really meaningful stuff of life, as I formerly thought. Our work itself is meaningful, because it is a place into which God has called us to bring his glory.

This is true of our work. It is also true of our families, our communities, our hobbies, and every other part of life. We glorify God by living in relationship with him and then living as expressions of his glory in every other relationship we have and every task to which we set our hands. Glorifying God is all-encompassing for those who see and share in his glory. At creation, this was his design.

CONCLUSION: WELCOMED INTO THE CELEBRATION

Why did God create? He created for his glory. That simple statement encapsulates what the Scriptures reveal about God's commitment to fill everything with the best of everything—with life and joy, thriving and flourishing, goodness and love. Creation is about his commitment to fill the earth with his glory.

That's where the story of the Bible begins and where it is pointing. It's the story of a great celebration. God the Father, Son, and Spirit, eternally celebrating how wonderful, how happy it is to be full of the glory of God.

It's the story of creation, as God determines to spread the celebration, inviting humans into the wonderful celebration shared between Father, Son, and Spirit. Those he creates as his image now get to participate in seeing and celebrating God's glory. They get to share in the joy of being like him. And they get to join God in spreading his celebration throughout creation, causing the celebration to grow until the whole earth is filled with his glory, and everything in creation redounds with glory to the Father, and to the Son, and to the Holy Spirit, world without end.

Chapter Two

GLORY LOST IN THE FALL

For all have sinned and fall short of the glory of God.

ROMANS 3:23

THERE'S AN EARLY JEWISH and Christian tradition that teaches that in the Garden of Eden, Adam and Eve were clothed with God's glory. Some texts say that their skin actually radiated light. The tradition presents a helpful picture of God's intention for human beings, whom he created as his images: we were to shine with his glory, so to speak, reflecting his character and nature, radiating his goodness and love as we ruled as his representatives over creation.

The theme of God's glory in the Bible, we have seen, is about God's intention to reveal his character and nature *to* and *through* humanity, filling the earth with his glory. From their unique relationship with God, humans, created in God's image, were to exercise Godlike dominion, spreading his glory through all creation. However, God's glory project in the world is barely underway when the story takes a tragic turn. Genesis 3 records the fall of humanity—the disobedience of Adam and Eve. This chapter of the Bible's story, and all that comes in its wake, makes plain that *when we reject the revelation of God's glory to us, we forfeit the revelation of his glory through us.*

DEPRIVED OF GLORY

When you get a sense of the goodness that God intended for his world, it is hard not to have a corresponding sense that something disastrous occurred and something precious was lost in the fall. But what exactly? According to the ancient tradition I mentioned, when Adam and Eve chose to disobey God and eat from the tree of the knowledge of good and evil, they lost their radiant glory. In one early Jewish book, after eating the forbidden fruit, Eve cries to the serpent, "Why have you done this to me, in that you have deprived me of the glory with which I was clothed?" She then persuades Adam to eat the fruit, and after doing so, he chastises his wife: "What have I done to you, that you have deprived me of the glory of God?"[1]

Many similar Jewish and Christian texts describe a loss of the glory of God as a consequence of Adam and Eve's sin. This led to shame at their nakedness and attempts to hide their glory-less condition by covering themselves with leaves. The tradition vividly communicates that something significant has been lost as a result of the fall, and the loss has to do with glory.

The apostle Paul similarly relates the sin of human beings with a loss of glory, though he does not have physical luminescence in mind. Three statements in the early chapters of Romans are especially relevant:

> For although they knew God, *they did not glorify him as God* or give thanks to him, but they became futile in their thinking, and their foolish hearts were darkened. (Rom 1:21 ESV altered)

> Claiming to be wise, they became fools, and *exchanged the glory of the immortal God* for images resembling mortal man and birds and animals and creeping things. (Rom 1:22-23)

> For all have sinned and *fall short of the glory of God*. (Rom 3:23)

We will give more attention to these verses and to Paul's understanding of the glory of God later in this study, but for now I simply wish to note that when Paul reads the creation and fall narratives, he sees them as having to do with glory given and glory lost.

---

[1]Apocalypse of Moses 20:3, 6. The Apocalypse of Moses, also known as the Life of Adam and Eve, is usually dated to the first century AD. This early Jewish text is not part of Scripture, but it provides a helpful window into the way some readers were interpreting the early Genesis narratives.

Our aim in this chapter is to explore how the fall affects the theme of God's glory revealed to and through humanity. To do this, we will begin in the Garden of Eden, with the revelation of God's glory there, and then see how the goodness of glory in the garden turned into a story of glory tragically distorted and lost.

GLORY IN THE GARDEN

After God creates and commissions humans in Genesis 1:28, he speaks for the tenth and final time in the Genesis 1 creation narrative:

> Then God said, "I give you every seed-bearing plant on the face of the whole earth and every tree that has fruit with seed in it. They will be yours for food. And to all the beasts of the earth and all the birds in the sky and all the creatures that move along the ground—everything that has the breath of life in it—I give every green plant for food." And it was so. (Gen 1:29-30 NIV)

Part of creation's purpose is to provide a home and sustenance for the creatures God has made. Immediately following the gift of God's provision for his creatures comes the affirmation of creation as "very good" (Gen 1:31). Creation is suited for the purpose intended by God—a dual purpose, as biblical scholar Scott Hafemann observes. Its immediate function is to provide for humanity, but its ultimate purpose is to reveal God's character: "The text makes clear that the function of creation is to provide a home and food for mankind as a manifestation of the perfection of our Provider."[2]

The early chapters of Genesis reveal that God is Creator and King over his creation. They also show the *kind* of Creator and King he is. By his acts in history, including his work of creation, God reveals his glory, making his character and nature known.

When we come to Genesis 2, we are given an inside look at the home God prepares for the first humans and at the way his glory is expressed in this home. The story is well-known. God creates the first human from the dust of the ground. God breathes into the man his very breath, sharing God's own life with him (Gen 2:7). God then plants a garden in Eden and places the man there (Gen 2:8).

---

[2]Scott J. Hafemann, *The God of Promise and the Life of Faith: Understanding the Heart of the Bible* (Wheaton, IL: Crossway, 2001), 29.

We find the Lord's abundant provision for his people at every turn in this story. God fills the garden with "every tree that is pleasant to the sight and good for food" (Gen 2:9). A river flows from Eden and waters the garden (Gen 2:10). This description—trees that are well-watered by rivers—becomes an image of flourishing and fruitfulness for later biblical authors (see, e.g., Ps 1:3; 104:16; Is 41:18-19; Jer 17:8; Ezek 47:7, 12). The garden is portrayed as a place of abundance and life, reflecting God's own fullness and life now shared with his people.

THE BEGINNINGS OF GODLIKE DOMINION

In this place of God's lavish abundance, Adam begins to rule over and care for creation, an important aspect of the glory with which God crowned humanity (Gen 1:26-28; Ps 8:5). Adam is tasked with *working* and *keeping* the garden (Gen 2:15), cultivating and drawing out life from the earth. Biblical scholars commonly note that the words translated "to work" (*'ābad*, "to work, serve") and "to keep" (*šāmar*, "to keep, guard") are used together later in the Bible with reference to the Levites (see Num 3:5-10; 8:26, 18:4-6). The Levites were one of the twelve tribes of Israel. Their job was to *serve* (*'ābad*) Aaron and his sons (the priests, who were also from the tribe of Levi) and to *guard* (*šāmar*) the tabernacle (the sacred dwelling place of God), protecting it from outsiders who might come near to defile it (Num 3:10).

The significance of this verbal connection between Adam and the Levites comes into focus in Genesis 3 when an outsider does in fact appear in the garden, the original sacred dwelling place of God. An aspect of Adam's image-bearing dominion over the creatures, it seems, was to guard the sacred space of Eden from outsiders such as the serpent, as his vocation to "work and keep" the garden suggests.

In the Garden of Eden, God gives a command to the man: "*Eat* of every tree of the garden" (Gen 2:16). The command is not first a negative command ("Don't eat!"), as we tend to think, but a positive one (*Eat freely!*). The tone "is that of fullness of permission. God is presented as the God of superabundance. God even *commands* this permission."[3] The trees and their fruit are

---

[3]Peter J. Gentry and Stephen J. Wellum, *Kingdom Through Covenant: A Biblical-Theological Understanding of the Covenants*, 2nd ed. (Wheaton, IL: Crossway, 2018), 667n29.

gifts from God. He made them spring up from the ground. And he made them "pleasant to the sight and good for food" (Gen 2:9). As with every part of God's creation, they are made to reflect God's glory, communicating something of his character and nature.

To enjoy God's creation and to fulfill the royal vocation he gave them, God's people must trust and obey him, remaining in right relationship with God. Hence the second part of his command: "But of the tree of the knowledge of good and evil you shall not eat, for in the day that you eat of it you shall surely die" (Gen 2:17). The implication, which becomes even more explicit as the story unfolds, is that humans can truly reflect and represent God in their dominion over creation (the *vocational* aspect of the glory God has shared with them) only when they rightly relate to God through trust and obedience (maintaining the *relational* aspect of their glory).

Following his command to Adam, the Lord declares something that, after the chain of "It was good" statements in Genesis 1, stands out in striking contrast: "It is not good that the man should be alone" (Gen 2:18). The Lord presents the animals to Adam, who, as God's representative, names them, much as God named the parts of his creation in Genesis 1.[4] But Adam realizes there is no suitable counterpart for him. To truly fulfill the commission given to humans—to subdue the earth and have dominion over it (Gen 1:26, 28)—Adam will need a helper (Gen 2:18). So, the Lord creates a woman, taken from the man's own flesh and bone, and presents her to him in a beautiful scene that ends with the pronouncement that "the man and his wife were both naked and were not ashamed" (Gen 2:25).

THE GARDEN AS A PLACE OF ACCESS TO GOD'S GLORY

The Garden of Eden provides a glimpse of what God ultimately intends for all creation. Here creation manifests the glory of God's goodness and generosity. Here humans rule over and care for creation in the way God intended for them. And here, in the Garden of Eden, God dwells with his people, granting them access to his presence and glory.

---

[4] Whatever Adam "called" (*qārā'*) them became their name (Gen 2:19), just as God "called" (*qārā'*) parts of creation day and night, heaven, earth, and seas (Gen 1:5, 8, 10).

We see this as God comes to walk in the garden in the cool of the day and to meet with the humans there (Gen 3:8-9). The same verb used in Genesis 3:8 for God *walking* (*hālak*) in the garden is used to describe the divine presence among the people of Israel, when God came to dwell among them in the tabernacle and, later, the temple (Lev 26:12, Deut 23:14, 2 Sam 7:6-7). God tells Israel, "I will make my dwelling among you, . . . and I will *walk* [*hālak*] among you and will be your God, and you shall be my people" (Lev 26:11-12). God's dwelling place within Israel, we will see later in our study, is meant to reflect the Garden of Eden and the fellowship and access to God that his people had there. Implied in all of this is a foundational truth, one that becomes a major theme in the story line of Scripture. God desires to dwell among his people. He desires close fellowship with them. He desires that they have access to his presence and glory. The text points to this as the way things were in the garden, before the fall. At the end of Genesis 2, the stage is set for humans to begin filling the earth with image bearers who will bring God's glory from the garden to the whole world.

DISTORTING GOD'S GLORY

Of course, before that happens, a devastating turn in the story occurs. The serpent, "more crafty than any other beast of the field that the LORD God had made" (Gen 3:1), comes on the scene. We're not told anything more about his origin or identity, but it becomes clear that this serpent is not a harmless garden snake. In his helpful study *Dominion and Dynasty*, Stephen Dempster says, "The snake is a bizarre aberration in the garden, with its ability to do what only humans and God can do (namely speak) and its attempt to rule the rulers."[5]

The issue of who will rule—and how—takes center stage in Genesis 3. God has shared his authority over creation with humans. But humans have a choice regarding how they will express that authority. God gives the command regarding the tree of the knowledge of good and evil in Genesis 2:16 in order to direct Adam in his dominion. Humans can reign through obedience to God, enabling them to reflect his image and glory into all creation.

---

[5]Stephen Dempster, *Dominion and Dynasty: A Biblical Theology of the Hebrew Bible*, New Studies in Biblical Theology (Downers Grove, IL: IVP Academic, 2003), 67.

Or they can choose to rule in their own autonomous way, apart from God, causing them to bring death into the world.

The serpent makes God's command the subject of his conversation with the woman in Genesis 3:1, "Did God actually say, 'You shall not eat of any tree in the garden'?" The tone and implication in the serpent's words are hard to miss. "What kind of God is he, really?" The serpent aims to disrupt Adam and Eve's relationship with God and to bring the humans, who were created to rule over God's creation, under his own rule. He does this is by presenting a counterview of God's character.

The serpent's question to the woman in Genesis 3:1 portrays God in a very different light from the way God has revealed himself in Genesis 2. He insinuates that God is stingy and close-fisted rather than generous and kind. When the woman counters his statement and aims to correct his distortion of God's command, the serpent responds once more with an attack on God's word and his revealed character: "But the serpent said to the woman, 'You will not surely die. For God knows that when you eat of it your eyes will be opened, and you will be like God, knowing good and evil'" (Gen 3:4-5).

His words suggest that God is withholding something good. God cannot be trusted. Perhaps he isn't as good or generous as Eve thought. The serpent's words, it appears, are enough to make Eve reconsider what she knows to be true of God, and therefore to reconsider what to do with God's command. Suddenly, as a result of the conversation with the serpent, she views the tree of the knowledge of good and evil as desirable, even necessary, to obtain what is good and will lead to wisdom, enabling her to "be like God, knowing good and evil" (Gen 3:5).

The description of what Eve saw when she looked at the tree of the knowledge of good and evil, namely that it was "good for food, and that it was a delight to the eyes" (Gen 3:6), is nearly identical to the author's description of all the other trees of the garden in Genesis 2. God did not give his people distasteful trees for food while withholding the best from them. All of the trees were "pleasant to the sight and good for food" (Gen 2:9), gifts from a good and generous God.

But Eve embraced the lie that to obey God's command would mean missing out on something good. Martin Luther once said, "The sin underneath all our sins is to trust the lie of the serpent that we cannot trust the love and grace of Christ and must take matters into our own hands." That lie took root in Eve's heart and in all her offspring after her. It is the lie that God is not good, that he cannot be trusted, that he does not have our best interests at heart, and that if we obey him, we will miss out on something necessary to our fulfillment and happiness. Behind the fall lies a distortion of the graciousness of God. Eve began to have a wrong view of God's character, leading to her distrust and disobedience.

"THEY DID NOT GLORIFY HIM AS GOD"

The root of Adam and Eve's sin in the garden, then, is their failure to respond appropriately to the revelation of God's glory given to them. The apostle Paul will later say, "Although they knew God, they did not glorify him as God or give thanks to him" (Rom 1:21 ESV altered). When Paul looks at "all the ungodliness and unrighteousness of men" (Rom 1:18), he sees it through the story of the first sin and the way this sin gets repeated with the people of Israel and then with all humanity. The fall, as with so many aspects of the early Genesis narrative, sets a pattern for what will continue to play out in human history. Or, to say it differently, the seeds of Genesis 1–3 grow and fill the story of the Bible.[6]

Presented with the abundance of the garden, Eve and "her husband who was with her" (Gen 3:6) did not give thanks for the good gifts God had provided. They did not respond to the revelation of God's glory in the garden by glorifying him through their trust and obedience. Rather, they became convinced that they could have something more and better if they chose to determine good and evil for themselves rather than trusting God as the source of their wisdom, the one who defines what is good and what is not. They chose to rule in their own way rather than ruling with and under the wisdom and authority of God.

Paul again expresses the essence of human sin, in the garden and beyond: "Claiming to be wise, they became fools, and exchanged the glory of the immortal God for images resembling mortal man and birds and animals and

---

[6]I heard G. K. Beale use this helpful image in a lecture he once delivered.

creeping things" (Rom 1:22-23).[7] Adam and Eve exchanged the glory of God—the truth about who he is and what he is like—for a lie (see Rom 1:25).

The effects of this exchange of God's glory were disastrous. Their eyes were opened, as the serpent said they would be, but not in a good way. The man and woman became aware of their nakedness and sought to cover the shame they now felt (Gen 3:7). When God came to walk in the cool of the garden with them, "the man and his wife hid themselves from the presence of the LORD God" (Gen 3:8). We find in this statement the central problem that results from the fall, which God, in the rest of the Bible, will set out to overcome. God's people have been separated from him, cut off from the relationship with him that they were created for. Now, instead of access to God's presence and fellowship with him, Adam and Eve's relationship with God is marked by fear and hiding from his face.[8]

NO LONGER SEEING OR SPREADING THE GLORY OF GOD

We have seen that the glory God bestowed on his images in creation has relational, vocational, and ethical aspects—sons and daughters of God, representative kings and queens, reflecting Godlike character into the world. Returning to the diagram I introduced earlier, we can express the immediate effects of the fall like this:

A. As a result of Adam and Eve's disobedience to God, their relationship with God has been broken. Humans no longer see God's glory rightly. And they no longer respond by glorifying God through gratitude, trust, and obedience but rather choose autonomy and disobedience.

---

[7]Paul seems to have both the fall of humanity in Gen 1–3 and Israel's sin and idolatry with the golden calf incident in Ex 32 in view in Rom 1:19-25, as the phrases "claiming to be wise, they became fools" (see Gen 3:6) and "[they] exchanged the glory of the immortal God" (see Ps 106:20) show. The story of the Bible presents both of these falls—Adam's and Israel's—as cut from the same cloth, so to speak, and as representative of the sin of all human beings after them.

[8]The Hebrew text says that Adam and Eve hid from God's "face" (*pānîm*). We will see in the following chapters how Moses closely associates God's face and his glory. To directly look on God's face is to behold the fullness of his glory (Ex 33:18-23). This is an experience Adam and Eve enjoyed prior to the fall but lost as a result of their sin.

Figure 2.1. The Fall results in humans having a broken relationship with God

B. A broken relationship with God leads to broken expressions of the ethical and vocational aspects of human glory into the world. Humans no longer extend God's rule and reign throughout creation through dominion that reflects God's self-giving love and brings life and blessing to the world. Because humanity rejects the revelation of God's glory to them, they forfeit the revelation of God's glory through them.

Figure 2.2. The Fall results in humans becoming broken reflections of God's glory

BROKEN RELATIONSHIPS AFTER THE FALL

Adam and Eve's sin sets the human story on a very different trajectory from the one for which they were created. Instead of filling the earth with human representatives who know and love God and who reflect his glory in the world, Adam and Eve and their offspring after them begin to fill the earth with shame, violence, corruption, and death. As Dane Ortlund puts it, "In

Adam, all sinned, and the tragic result is that the divine glory with which humanity was vested in Eden . . . went into meltdown."[9]

This meltdown is what we see as we continue to read the story after the fall. People were created for relationship—with God, with other humans, and with creation. The story after the fall is a story of broken relationships—between humans and with creation, both of which flow out of our broken relationship with God.

Adam's relationship with his wife is immediately marked by blame and self-preservation rather than self-giving love: "The woman whom you gave to be with me, she gave me fruit of the tree, and I ate" (Gen 3:12). God's words to the woman in Genesis 3:16 recall his commission given to humans in Genesis 1:28, but now the commission has acquired new and painful elements. Multiplying images to fill the earth will come through a multiplication of pain. And the responsibility to rule over creation will tempt humans to subdue one another in ways not reflective of God's loving care (Gen 3:16).[10] When we no longer trust God's graciousness and see his glory rightly, it causes us to become takers rather than givers, self-protectors rather than outwardly focused lovers. Sadly, this has been the story of human relationships from Eden onward.

Additionally, instead of ruling over and caring for creation in a way that brings flourishing and abundance, now the man's relationship with the created world will be marked by painful toil and strife, by "thorns and thistles" (Gen 3:18). Made to flourish under Godlike kingship expressed through humans, creation is instead under a curse (Gen 5:29). When the first humans turned from God's glory, there were cosmic implications. Sin affected the whole created order, resulting in a creation in bondage to corruption (see Rom 8:19-21) rather than a creation dripping with the glory of God under the rule and reign of glory-spreading, image-bearing kings and queens.

---

[9]Dane C. Ortlund, "What Does It Mean to Fall Short of the Glory of God? Romans 3:23 in Biblical-Theological Perspective," *Westminster Theological Journal* 80, no. 1 (2018): 139.

[10]Mitchell L. Chase, *Short of Glory: A Biblical and Theological Exploration of the Fall* (Wheaton, IL: Crossway, 2023), 136.

GLORY-LESS LIFE OUTSIDE THE GARDEN

In response to their sin, God sends the human couple out of the garden, away from his presence and away from the tree of life (Gen 3:23-24). Humans continue to be God's image in the world. God's words to Noah after the flood affirm this, as he tells Noah that he will require a reckoning when the blood of humans is shed, "for God made man in his own image" (Gen 9:6). We read of continued outworkings of dominion, as humans build families and cities and societies and technologies. A genealogy in Genesis 5, for example, tells of individuals who develop the practices of animal husbandry, playing musical instruments, and metalworking (Gen 5:20-22). A later genealogy notes that Nimrod was a mighty hunter and a builder of cities (Gen 10:9-14). In one sense, these are expressions of the vocation God gave to humans as his image.

Adam and Eve's offspring continue to create and exercise dominion in numerous ways, but much of it is devoid of God's glory, and is marked instead by violence, corruption, and selfish pursuits at the expense of others. It is the character of humans in ruling the world that represents God.[11] After the fall, humans fail to reflect God's character and to bring his self-giving love into the world. They do just the opposite, expressing God's image in broken and distorted ways.

SPREADING DEATH INSTEAD OF LIFE

Outside the garden, broken expressions of God's image and glory multiply rapidly. Cain spitefully kills his brother Abel (Gen 4:8). Not long after, Lamech flaunts his own violent murder of another man (Gen 4:23).

Banished from God's presence, away from the tree of life, humans are destined to die, just as God said they would (see Gen 2:17). Not only do they die individually, but they also inflict death on one another and on all creation. As a result of their sin, they bring the power of death into the world in place of the life-giving reign they were intended to bring.

The genealogy in Genesis 5 punctuates the reality of death in God's world as a consequence for sin. The story of each person listed in the genealogy (with the exception of Enoch, who "walked with God, and he was not, for

---

[11]Gentry and Wellum, *Kingdom Through Covenant*, 236.

God took him," Gen 5:24) ends the same, stark way: "and he died" (see Gen 5:5, 8, 11, 14, 17-18, 25, 31). Well did Paul say that "because of one man's trespass, death *reigned*" (Rom 5:17).

Picture the opening scene to Disney's *The Lion King*. It's a scene of celebration, as all the animals of the Pride Lands make their way to the presentation of the newborn lion cub, Mufasa's son, heir to the throne. The scene is full of color and life—green grass and trees, flowing rivers, and brightly colored animals full of joy and celebration. This is the Pride Lands under Mufasa's good rule.

Now picture the Pride Lands after Mufasa is killed and the evil Scar usurps the throne. Under Scar's selfish rule, everything green and full of life dries up and withers, turning to dusty, dingy brown. Food becomes scarce. Death and despair are everywhere. It's a picture, in Disney animation, of "thorns and thistles" (Gen 3:18), of "you shall surely die" (Gen 2:17), of ground that is under a curse (Gen 5:29). It's a picture of what happens to the world under the reign of human beings who no longer rule with God's generous character and fill the earth with his glory.

FILLING THE EARTH, BUT NOT WITH GLORY

Genesis 3 presents the first and inaugural fall from glory. But the following chapters of the Bible recount additional falls, as humanity continues to spiral downward in their rebellion against God. Two rebellions receive focused attention.

The first comes in Genesis 6, when the "sons of God" take the "daughters of man" as wives. Setting aside the debate about who these sons of God are, it is important to see that the author presents their sinful actions in a way that is intended to evoke the sin of Genesis 3. Just as Eve *saw* that the tree was *good* for food and *took* and ate (Gen 3:6), so the sons of God *saw* that the daughters of man were *good* and *took* as their wives any they chose (Gen 6:2). The identical language—*saw, good, took*—shows that we are witnessing another iteration of the sin of the garden.

This connection to Genesis 3 is only the beginning of allusions the author makes in this passage to the previous Genesis narrative. There are also several explicit verbal links to the commission of Genesis 1:28. Genesis 6 opens by telling us that the events take place "when man began to *multiply* on the face of the land" (Gen 6:1). There is a sense in which Genesis 1:28 is happening, but there is another sense in which it is definitely not. Though humans have *multiplied* (the same word that is used in Gen 1:28), they have not filled the earth with God's glory. Rather, "The LORD saw that the wickedness of man was great in the earth, and that every intention of the thoughts of his heart was only evil continually" (Gen 6:5). This is the opposite of what humans were made for. Created to reflect God's goodness, righteousness, and self-giving love into the world, wickedness and evil have filled men's hearts instead. As a result, "the earth was *filled* with violence" (Gen 6:11, 13).

There is another significant connection to the creation narrative in the way the author tells this story. In Genesis 6:12, the author alludes to the pronouncement that God's creation was "very good" (Gen 1:31), showing that the opposite is now true as a result of human sin and rebellion. The verses, when set alongside each other, show the verbal similarities:

And God saw *everything that he had made,* and behold, **it was very good**. (Gen 1:31)

And God saw *the earth,* and behold, **it was corrupt**. (Gen 6:12)

In place of God's very good creation, the earth is now *corrupt*—destroyed or ruined, as the Hebrew verb indicates—because *violence* has filled it (Gen 6:11, 13). "Instead of the glory of God being everywhere," Dempster says, "it is *ḥāmās* ('violence') that is omnipresent."[12]

Through the flood, God wipes his creation clean in judgment, returning it to the precreation chaos of Genesis 1:2. Then, through Noah and his family, God brings about the beginnings of a new creation. God recommissions them, giving them the same command as at creation: "And God blessed Noah and his sons and said to them, 'Be fruitful and multiply and fill the earth'" (Gen 9:1). God affirms that humans are to continue to rule over his creation, though now there is an aspect of fear and dread that will mark their relationship to the creatures over which they rule (Gen 9:2). He affirms that humans are still

---

[12]Dempster, *Dominion and Dynasty*, 72.

his image (Gen 9:6). They are to multiply and spread his glory throughout the world, as was their vocation from the beginning.

This brings us to a second story, which captures another tragic act of rebellion against God and against his good purposes for his world.

A NAME FOR OURSELVES

The story of the tower of Babel comes sandwiched between two genealogies of Shem (Gen 10:21-32; 11:10-32). Shem was one of Noah's sons, the one from whom the nation of Israel will descend. Significantly, Shem, in Hebrew, means "name," which is what the story of Babel is all about.

We are told that the whole earth had one language, and as people migrated from the east, they found a plain in the land of Shinar and settled there (Gen 11:1-2). They developed bricks, burning them thoroughly and using bitumen for mortar (Gen 11:3). On display is another example of human dominion and creativity. But instead of offering up the work of their hands in love and service to God, using it in ways that bring blessing and life, they do just the opposite. "Then they said, 'Come, let us build ourselves a city and a tower with its top in the heavens, and let us make a name for ourselves, lest we be dispersed over the face of the whole earth'" (Gen 11:4).

In a rebellious bid for autonomy reminiscent of Eden, the people aim to use their God-given authority and creative capacity to act against God's purposes. In the Bible, to name something is often an expression of authority (as we see in God's naming the parts of creation in Gen 1 and in Adam's naming the animals in Gen 2). A name also gives a sense of identity and significance. God is the one who names his people, who marks them as his and gives them their identity, significance, and purpose. At Babel, though, the people want to "make a name for [themselves]" (Gen 11:4) rather than being under God's authority and receiving their identity and significance from him.

Their stated reason for desiring this is "lest we be dispersed over the face of the earth." This is an act of direct rebellion against God's commission given to humanity in Genesis 1:28 (and reaffirmed following the flood in Gen 9:1). They do not want to fill the earth with God's image and glory, and so they aim to build a city and a tower in order to establish their own autonomy and carry out their own purposes apart from God.

Theologian Henry Blocher refers to Genesis 11 as a sort of sequel to Genesis 3:

> By its calculated naivety and its play on words, the narrative of Genesis 11 bears an amazing resemblance to Genesis 3. It is basically the same project that mankind seeks to fulfil in the two chapters: to make himself equal with God and thereby gain autonomy. He wants to ascend to heaven, instead of filling the earth. He claims to make a name for himself, instead of receiving his name from his Maker.[13]

At Babel, we witness a loss of intended identity and a rejection of intended vocation. Created as God's image, humans are to celebrate *God's* greatness and reflect *his* glory.[14] But at Babel, the people reject the identity given them by God, opting to make a name for themselves instead. They also reject their vocation, refusing to rule as God's image and fill the earth with his glory.

In an act of merciful judgment, God confuses their language and "dispersed them from there over the face of all the earth" (Gen 11:8). As the narrative unfolds, we find that through Shem's line comes a man named Abram (later renamed Abraham by God). God appears to him and promises, "I will . . . make your name great, so that you will be a blessing" (Gen 12:2). This blessing recalls the one given in Genesis 1:28, when God blessed his people so that they might be fruitful and multiply and fill the earth, bringing his rule and reign to all creation. That blessing, God tells Abram, will come through *God* making Abram's name great (unlike the people's attempt at Babel to make a name for themselves).

What is remarkable in this story is that the rebellious people God disperses at Babel—who become the nations of the earth listed in Genesis 10—are the ones he intends to restore his blessing to through making Abram's name great: "In you all families of the earth shall be blessed" (Gen 12:3). In scattering the people at Babel, God puts them back on the path of redemption,

---

[13]Henri Blocher, *In the Beginning: The Opening Chapters of Genesis* (Leicester, UK: Inter-Varsity Press, 1984), 203.

[14]God's name refers to his character and is used interchangeably with his glory in certain contexts. See, e.g., Ex 33:18-19, 22; 34:5.

back in the path of his purposes. Though it will take time to unfold, Abraham and his seed (Gen 22:18) become the answer to the human problem. God's plan through Abraham is the very plan he instituted at creation. He intends to fill the earth with his glory through people who know him and have a special relationship with him. Those people, then, become the agents of God's blessing to the world, as God sets out to restore the goodness of his rule and reign through all the earth through their dominion as his image.

GOD'S GLORY IN RESPONSE TO HUMAN REBELLION

At every dark moment in the story of the Bible, we find God's glory on display, as he reveals his character, responding in judgment and mercy to the rebellion of his people. In Eden, God pronounces judgment on the serpent and promises to send a human who will triumph over this usurper (Gen 3:15)—a promise that grows into the messianic hopes of the rest of the Old Testament. Additionally, God graciously clothes his people, covering their shame, and sends them from the garden—an act of merciful judgment. No longer will God grant them direct access to his glory and presence, nor do they have access to the tree of life. Yet this act of judgment is at the same time a kindness, preventing man from living forever in the misery of their fallen state (Gen 3:22).

In the flood, God judges human wickedness, but he graciously saves Noah and his family: "But Noah found favor [*ḥēn*, 'grace'] in the eyes of the LORD" (Gen 6:8). Through Noah, God preserves his creation and reinitiates his plan and purpose for humanity and for the whole world.

At Babel, God disrupts the people's rebellious plans, bringing judgment on them and scattering them over the face of the earth. But he chooses a man, Abraham, to restore his blessing to the very people whom he scattered over the earth in response to their rebellious attempts to make a name for themselves.

God is just. And God is merciful. This is the essence of his glory, as he will later show to Moses (see Ex 34:6-7). The fall is a tragic story of God's glory rejected, human glory lost, and God's glory revealed at every turn. As the story continues, we will see how God continues to make his glory known and how he works through Abraham's descendants to fill the earth with his glory, just as he planned from the beginning.

CONCLUSION: THE STORY WITHOUT THE FALL

I once taught a biblical theology class to a group of men training to be pastors in Brazil. After we walked through the beautiful story of creation and of God's plan for his people to enjoy a relationship of loving intimacy with God, out of which would flow the spreading of God's glory throughout the earth, one of the students had tears in his eyes. He said to me, "Can we just stop here?" I asked, "What do you mean?" He responded, "It's so good. What God planned. What we were made for. It's so wonderful. But I know what comes next in the story. Can't we just stop here?" He didn't want to move on to the fall.

Of course, we did move on to the fall. It's in the Bible. And its effects are all around us. We can't skip it. We can't avoid it. So we began to walk through the ugliness of human rebellion in the Bible, the pain of life lived out of fellowship with God, and the plague of death sweeping over God's world. As we moved through the tragedy of the fall—of God's glory rejected and defaced, and of a world filled not with glory but with violence and evil and death—the student's tears became sobs. It was a sad but sweet moment as the Holy Spirit gave him a sense of the goodness of God's glory revealed to and through humanity and filling creation, and the horror of its loss.

In creation, God shared his eternal celebration—the glory enjoyed by Father, Son, and Holy Spirit—with his people and his world. The fall seemed to bring an end to the celebration on earth. The joy and happiness, so sweet and full for a moment, were spoiled.

But the story isn't over. In God's unfolding plan, the fall becomes the occasion for God to reveal himself in new and more brilliant shades of glory. And so the fall itself, and all our human sin and rebellion, becomes a servant to God's plan to wonderfully make his glory known in all the earth.

Chapter Three

GLORY TO AND THROUGH ISRAEL, PART ONE

You are My Servant, Israel,
In whom I will show My glory.

ISAIAH 49:3 NASB

THE FALL LEAVES US with a question: Can glory be restored? God's glory to and through his people, and his glory filling the whole world? Is this plan and purpose of God a failed plan, abandoned and left lying in the dust from which Adam was formed and to which he will now return (Gen 3:19)? God's response to the fall offers a resounding answer: his glory can and will be restored to his people, and his glory will fill the earth. The answer comes in multiple forms.

GOD HAS NOT ABANDONED HIS PLAN

In response to Adam's sin and subjugation to the serpent, God becomes the first evangelist, the first preacher of good news. To the serpent, God says,

> I will put enmity between you and the woman,
>> and between your offspring and her offspring;

> he shall bruise your head,
>> and you shall bruise his heel. (Gen 3:15)

This declaration has come to be known as the *protoevangelium*, the first gospel. God will raise up offspring from the woman who will do battle with and triumph over the serpent. This veiled and mysterious promise, we find as the Bible's story continues, is about God restoring to humans the dominion he always intended for them. As Stephen Dempster says, "The seed of woman will restore lost glory. Human—and therefore divine—dominion will be established over the world."[1]

There are other indications in the text of Genesis that God has not abandoned his plan to fill the earth with his glory. God's glory-oriented commission to humanity in Genesis 1:28 follows these important words: "And God blessed them" (Gen 1:28). The commission flows out of and is enabled by the blessing of God. It is significant, then, that when God first speaks to Abraham (Gen 12:1-3), just after the scattering of the nations at Babel (Gen 10–11), the encounter centers on God's blessing. In fact, the word *bless* or *blessing* occurs five times in these verses: "I will *bless* you . . . so that you will be a *blessing*. I will *bless* those who *bless* you . . . and in you all the families of the earth shall be *blessed*."

It is noteworthy that the word *curse*, which in Scripture is the opposite of *bless*, occurs precisely five times in Genesis 1–11 (Gen 3:14, 17; 4:11; 5:29; 9:25). To our way of thinking and reading Scripture, this may seem merely coincidental. But such numerical correlations are a common way the biblical authors make significant theological points. Through the fivefold repetition of the word *bless*, the author of Genesis makes the subtle but powerful point that God's blessing to and through Abraham is the divine answer to the curse introduced by the fall. Through Abraham and his offspring, God will restore the blessing of Genesis 1:28 to "all the families of the earth" (Gen 12:3).

In addition to this, a "Genesis 1:28 trail" runs through the rest of the book. The terms and concepts—bless, be fruitful, multiply, fill the earth, and

---

[1]Stephen Dempster, *Dominion and Dynasty: A Biblical Theology of the Hebrew Bible*, New Studies in Biblical Theology (Downers Grove, IL: IVP Academic, 2003), 69.

dominion—show up time and again, as God reaffirms his purpose for his people, the same purpose given to humanity from the very beginning.[2] The repetition is striking, as table 3.1 shows.

Table 3.1. The repetition of Genesis 1:28

Noah and his sons	Genesis 9:1, 7	Be fruitful; multiply; fill the earth
Abraham	Genesis 12:2-3	Bless; all . . . the earth
	Genesis 17:2, 6, 8	Multiply; fruitful; give land (= fill the earth)
	Genesis 22:17-28	Bless, multiply, defeat enemies (= dominion)
Isaac	Genesis 26:3-4	Bless; give land (= fill the earth); multiply
	Genesis 26:22, 24	Be fruitful; bless; multiply
Jacob	Genesis 28:3-4	Bless; fruitful; multiply; give land (= fill the earth)
	Genesis 35:11-12	Be fruitful; multiply; give land (= fill the earth)
	Genesis 47:27 (including Jacob's sons)	Fruitful; multiply
	Genesis 48:3-4	Fruitful; multiply; give land (= fill the earth)

N. T. Wright comments that through the reiteration of these terms and ideas at key moments, the narrative quietly makes the point that Abraham and his family inherit the role God gave to Adam and Eve and their offspring at creation.[3] But, as Wright notes, there are significant differences. The command to "be fruitful" has in most cases turned into a promise: "I will make you fruitful." The word *exceedingly* is added in Genesis 17: "I will make you *exceedingly* fruitful" (Gen 17:6; see Gen 17:2, which has "I will multiply you *greatly*"). The command to fill the earth now centers on the land God promises to give to Abraham and his offspring. And dominion over creation (Gen 1:26, 28) now focuses on supremacy over enemies. Wright concludes,

---

[2]Peter J. Gentry and Stephen J. Wellum, *Kingdom Through Covenant: A Biblical-Theological Understanding of the Covenants*, 2nd ed. (Wheaton, IL: Crossway, 2018), 261-63.
[3]N. T. Wright, *Climax of the Covenant: Christ and the Law in Pauline Theology* (London: T&T Clark, 1991), 22-23.

"We could sum up this aspect of Genesis by saying: Abraham's children are God's true humanity, and their homeland is the new Eden."[4]

God has not abandoned his purpose to fill the earth with his glory. Rather, he continually reaffirms his purpose as the story of the Bible unfolds.

GOD'S PLAN CONTINUES WITH ISRAEL

This brings us to the book of Exodus and the story of Abraham's descendants, the nation of Israel. With Israel we find another decisive declaration of *God's intent to reveal his glory to and through his people so that his glory will fill the world.*

Exodus opens by connecting the story back to the narrative of Genesis, recounting the descendants of Jacob who came to Egypt with him (Ex 1:1-6). Then it goes further, connecting these people to the purpose of God for humanity given in Genesis 1:28. The people of Israel, we are told, "were *fruitful* and increased greatly; they *multiplied* and grew exceedingly strong, so that *the land was filled* with them" (Ex 1:7). But instead of subduing the earth, they are subdued by the Egyptians (Ex 1:8-14). This is the backdrop to the revelation of God's glory that unfolds in the exodus from Egypt and the covenant God makes with Israel at Mount Sinai.

In this chapter and the next, we will journey through Exodus, exploring how the story of Israel contributes to the glory theme in the Bible. We will begin our journey by jumping ahead to an important passage that recounts God's definitive self-revelation of his glory in the Old Testament, Exodus 33:18–34:7. Then we will back up and follow Israel's story through the book of Exodus to see what led up to this important moment when God made his glory known.

"SHOW ME YOUR GLORY"

In Exodus 33:18, Moses makes a remarkable request of God: "Please show me your glory." In time we will come to the wider context of this passage, and we will see why Moses made this request in the first place. But for now I want to focus on the nature of Moses' request and especially on God's response to Moses.

---

[4]Wright, *Climax of the Covenant*, 23.

Moses has seen various manifestations of God's glory already. God has revealed his glory through signs and wonders in Egypt, through mighty acts of deliverance, through miraculous provision in the wilderness, and in visible splendor in the burning bush and in the pillar of cloud and fire. The people witnessed God's glory on Mount Sinai from afar, but Moses went up on the mountain to meet with God and actually entered the glory cloud (Ex 19:20; 24:15-18). On top of all this, we are told, "The LORD used to speak to Moses face to face, as a man speaks to his friend" (Ex 33:11). If anyone has seen and experienced God's glory, it is Moses. In Exodus 33, though, Moses asks for something more, an even greater experience of God's glory than he has previously known. It seems the more you behold and experience God's glory, the more of his glory you crave.

God responds favorably to Moses, and his response sheds light on just what God's glory *is*: "And he said, 'I will make all my goodness pass before you and will proclaim before you my name "The LORD." And I will be gracious to whom I will be gracious, and will show mercy on whom I will show mercy. But,' he said, 'you cannot see my face, for man shall not see me and live'" (Ex 33:19-20). The first thing to notice is that Moses asks to see God's *glory* (Ex 33:18), and God responds by saying that he will make his *goodness* pass before Moses and will proclaim his *name* before him (Ex 33:19). Are God's goodness and his name in some sense related to or perhaps synonymous with his glory? Or are they different from his glory, a consolation prize, as if God were saying, "I won't show you my glory, but I'll show you my goodness and proclaim my name to you instead"? The answer comes just a few verses later: "And the LORD said, 'Behold, there is a place by me where you shall stand on the rock, and *while my glory passes by* I will put you in a cleft of the rock, and I will cover you with my hand until I have passed by. Then I will take away my hand, and you shall see my back, but my face shall not be seen'" (Ex 33:21-23).

To make his goodness pass before Moses and to proclaim his name before him *is* to show Moses his glory. It's almost as if you can put an equal sign between God's glory, his goodness, and his name. Each of them is an expression of God's character and nature—his goodness, his essence, his name, his glory.

In response to Moses' request, God will show Moses who he is and what he is like in a way that surpasses the glory Moses has already seen. However, God tells Moses that he can't see his glory *directly*: "'But,' he said, 'you cannot see my face, for man shall not see me and live'" (Ex 33:20).

Even Moses' face-to-face talks with God (Ex 33:11) were mediated through the pillar of cloud (Ex 33:9), which served to veil God's face and protect his people from a direct encounter with his glory. Ever since sin entered the Garden of Eden, a direct experience of God's glory has been a terrifying prospect for humans, which is why Adam and Eve "hid themselves from the *face* of the LORD" (Gen 3:8, my translation). God's face, in Exodus 33:20, refers to his glory manifested in an unveiled way, like it was in the Garden of Eden, before humans rebelled against him. In a sinful, fallen state, humans can no longer be in the presence of God's glory in a direct way without being overwhelmed or consumed by his glory.

And so, God plans to put Moses in the cleft of a rock and to cover him with his hand so that Moses will be able to see only God's back and not his face (Ex 33:22-23). These anthropomorphisms (attributing human characteristics to God)—hand, back, face—convey that God will indeed give Moses a fuller glimpse of his glory than he has yet had, but he will also protect Moses from being consumed by this vision of his glory.

GOD REVEALS HIS GLORY

Moses has asked to see God's glory. And God has told Moses he will show him his glory. So at the invitation of God, Moses climbs Mount Sinai, and the Lord grants him his request:

> The LORD descended in the cloud and stood with him there, and proclaimed the name of the LORD. The LORD passed before him and proclaimed, "The LORD, the LORD, a God merciful and gracious, slow to anger, and abounding in steadfast love and faithfulness, keeping steadfast love for thousands, forgiving iniquity and transgression and sin, but who will by no means clear the guilty, visiting the iniquity of the fathers on the children and the children's children, to the third and the fourth generation." (Ex 34:5-7)

When God reveals his glory to Moses, this is what he reveals. This is his character and nature, who God is at the core of his being. God expresses his glory in mercy and compassion, loyal love and forgiveness toward those who don't deserve it but whom he nevertheless desires to give it. And he expresses his glory in justice—his commitment to not let his glory be disregarded and defaced, to not let everything good and beautiful be destroyed and evil go unchecked in his world forever.

God's mercy and justice are both aspects of the beautiful and harmonious glory of God. But you can almost feel the tension between them. The way this tension is resolved will come much later in the biblical story, on another mountain, where God will display the glory of his mercy and his justice as his Son hangs on a cross. But for now, God lets the tension stand, declaring to Moses his glory and goodness in his love, mercy, and forgiveness, and also in his justice.

It is hard to overstate the importance that this revelation of God's glory plays in the rest of the Bible. Its fingerprints are everywhere. Going forward, this becomes the reference point when people describe the Lord's character. It shows up in every major section of the Old Testament, from the Law, to the Prophets, to the Psalms and Writings. Each of them points back to this revelation of God's glory in various ways. David, for example, declares in the Psalms: "But you, O Lord, are a God merciful and gracious, slow to anger and abounding in steadfast love and faithfulness" (Ps 86:15). Jonah, knowing that God would act according to his character revealed to Moses, gives this as the reason he did not want to preach to Nineveh: "O LORD, is not this what I said when I was yet in my country? That is why I made haste to flee to Tarshish; for I knew that you are a gracious God and merciful, slow to anger and abounding in steadfast love, and relenting from disaster" (Jon 4:2). Likewise, the prophet Jeremiah declares: "You show steadfast love to thousands, but you repay the guilt of fathers to their children after them, O great and mighty God, whose name is the LORD of hosts" (Jer 32:18).

What is God like? He is merciful and forgiving, slow to anger, full of steadfast love for thousands of generations. And he is just, judging evil to the third and fourth generation for those who scorn his mercy and persist in their rebellion. We find in this declaration of God's glory an explicit expression of what God has shown his people from the very beginning, and which we saw in his response to the fall and the sin that followed in its wake in Genesis. God is merciful. God is just. This is God's glory.

To understand why this moment is so significant, we need to back up in the story to see what led to Moses' petition in the first place and how the revelation of God's glory to Moses and to Israel relates to the larger plan that God initiated at creation.

ISRAEL: GOD'S FIRSTBORN SON

In Exodus, God first appears to Moses on Mount Horeb (later called Mount Sinai) in a burning bush (Ex 3:1-6), a brilliant and fiery display of his glory that we see again and again in Exodus (Ex 13:21-22; 14:19-20, 24; 16:10; 19:9, 16; 24:15-16, 18; 33:9-10; 34:5; 40:34-38).

God makes his intention to rescue his people known to Moses and sends Moses back to Egypt with this message for Pharaoh: "Thus says the LORD, Israel is my firstborn son, and I say to you, 'Let my son go that he may serve me.' If you refuse to let him go, behold, I will kill your firstborn son" (Ex 4:22-23). The title "firstborn son" recalls the privileged status given to humanity in Genesis 1 and also foreshadows the coming deliverance of the Israelites through the Passover (Ex 12). Like the creation of humans as God's image (Gen 1:26), "firstborn son" carries connotations of both sonship and authority.[5] Think of monarchies through history. A king's greatest prize is his firstborn son, the one who will inherit the throne and exercise royal authority in the kingdom. Israel, as God's firstborn son, inherits the relationship and vocation intended for humans in creation. The nation of Israel is like a new, corporate Adam, a people whom God creates to know him in a special way and to make his character and nature known in the earth.

ISRAEL'S CREATION

The exodus from Egypt is a re-creation story, intentionally drawing our attention back to the first creation account. After the fall, re-creation comes through redemption, as we see in Israel's deliverance from bondage in Egypt.

In Genesis 1, creation is structured around ten powerful speech acts, as the ten occurrences of the phrase "And God said" show (Gen 1:3, 6, 9, 11, 14,

---

[5]In Ps 89:27, God appoints David his "firstborn son, the highest of the kings of the earth," a clear expression of the exalted status and royal overtones often associated with this title.

20, 24, 26, 28-29). Now, in Exodus, God's judgment on the Egyptians comes through ten plagues. These dramatic displays of God's power are acts of de-creation, much like the flood narrative of Genesis 7. In Genesis, God creates (Gen 1), decreates (Gen 7), then re-creates (Gen 8–9). Now, in Exodus, the decreation acts of the ten plagues are followed by a re-creation that, in subtle but distinct ways, parallels the Genesis 1 creation account.

When the Israelites come up to the edge of the Red Sea, the pillar of cloud—a physical manifestation of God's presence and glory that goes before the Isra-elites (Ex 13:21-22)—moves between them and the Egyptians (Ex 14:19-20). God causes darkness over Egypt, while the light of his glory shines on Israel: "And there was the cloud and the darkness. And it lit up the night without one coming near the other all night" (Ex 14:20). The scene recalls the first creation, when God "separated the light from the darkness" (Gen 1:4).[6]

Following the separation of light from darkness in the first creation ac-count, God separated the waters from the dry land (Gen 1:9-10). He did this again after the flood, when he caused the waters of the earth to recede so that dry land could emerge (Gen 8:3-12), enabling a new start for humanity. Now in the exodus, God divides the sea, once more revealing dry land and enabling new life to emerge through the waters (Ex 14:21-22).[7]

Significantly, in the Genesis 1 creation account, again at the flood, and now at the crossing of the Red Sea, God's "Spirit" or "wind" (*rûaḥ*, "spirit, wind, breath") is present and has a role in relation to the waters. In Genesis 1:2, God's Spirit (*rûaḥ*) was hovering over the face of the waters. Following the flood, God made a wind (*rûaḥ*) blow over the earth, causing the waters to subside (Gen 8:1). And in the exodus from Egypt, "the LORD drove the sea back by a strong east wind [*rûaḥ*] all night and made the sea dry land, and the waters were divided. And the people of Israel went into the midst of the sea on dry ground, the waters being a wall to them on their right hand and on their left" (Ex 14:21-22).[8]

---

[6]L. Michael Morales, *Exodus Old and New: A Biblical Theology of Redemption*, Essential Studies in Biblical Theology (Downers Grove, IL: IVP Academic, 2020), 50.

[7]Morales, *Exodus Old and New*, 50.

[8]The parting of the Red Sea is later referred to as "the blast of [the Lord's] nostrils" (Ex 15:8). Is 11:15 similarly speaks of a future deliverance of God's people and judgment on Egypt, in which "the LORD will utterly destroy the tongue of the Sea of Egypt, and will wave his hand over the River *with his scorching breath* [*rûaḥ*], . . . and he will lead people across in sandals."

These associations between creation and the exodus are perhaps what led the prophet Isaiah, many years later, to call the Lord "the Creator of Israel, your King" (Is 43:15), connecting the Lord, as Israel's Creator, directly to their deliverance through the Red Sea:

"I am the LORD, your Holy One,
      the *Creator of Israel, your King.*"
Thus says the LORD,
      who makes a way in the sea,
      a path in the mighty waters. . . .
for I give water in the wilderness,
      rivers in the desert,
to give drink to my chosen people,
      the people whom I formed for myself
      that they might declare my praise. (Is 43:15-17, 20-21)

For Isaiah, the creation of the people of Israel at the exodus (which happened several hundred years before Isaiah's time) becomes a picture of what God will do in Isaiah's own day by bringing Israel out of exile. Isaiah's words confirm that the redemption of Israel from Egypt is a new creation event. Through the exodus, God forms a people for a special relationship with himself and for a special purpose in his world. He creates a new, corporate Adam, a people whom he is bringing to Sinai, where they will worship him and behold his glory. And from there, he will lead them to Canaan, the Promised Land, which, like a new Eden, will be the special place where God will dwell with his people once more.

This is what the people of Israel celebrate in "the song of Moses," which they sing to the Lord following their deliverance through the sea: "You will bring them in and plant them on your own mountain, the place, O LORD, which you have made for your abode, the sanctuary, O Lord, which your hands have established" (Ex 15:17). Peter Gentry and Stephen Wellum comment, "In this verse the establishment of Israel in the land of Canaan is pictured as the planting of a tree in a *mountain sanctuary*, exactly the picture of Eden presented in Genesis 2 and Ezekiel 28."[9]

---

[9]Gentry and Wellum, *Kingdom Through Covenant*, 263.

Moses' song closes with a final declaration, "The LORD will reign forever and ever" (Ex 15:18). Israel's planting in the sanctuary of God goes hand in hand with the Lord's reign. By delivering Israel through his judgment on Egypt, God decisively displays his glory. He is King over all the earth. And as at creation, when the Lord purposed to spread the goodness of his reign through humans (see Gen 1:26-28), so now Israel's creation and vocation will be inseparably bound together.

THAT ALL THE EARTH MIGHT KNOW YAHWEH

Two divine purposes run beneath the events of the exodus from Egypt: (1) Israel will come to know Yahweh (Ex 6:6-7; 10:2), and (2) the nations will come to know Yahweh (Ex 7:5, 17; 8:10, 22; 9:14, 16, 29; 14:4, 17-18).

In this great act of deliverance, God is first revealing himself to his people, making his glory known to them. He sends Moses to the people with this message:

> Say therefore to the people of Israel, "I am the LORD, and I will bring you
> out from under the burdens of the Egyptians, and I will deliver you from
> slavery to them, and I will redeem you with an outstretched arm and with
> great acts of judgment. I will take you to be my people, and I will be your
> God, *and you shall know that I am the LORD your God*, who has brought you
> out from under the burdens of the Egyptians." (Ex 6:6-7)

"You shall know that I am the LORD" is a refrain that echoes throughout Israel's story. By his acts of mercy and judgment, God reveals who he is to his people.

But God's purpose goes beyond revealing himself only to the people of Israel. When Moses first came to Pharaoh with the message, "Thus says the LORD, the God of Israel, 'Let my people go, that they may hold a feast to me in the wilderness'" (Ex 5:1), Pharaoh responded arrogantly (or perhaps just honestly), "Who is the LORD, that I should obey his voice and let Israel go? I do not know the LORD, and moreover, I will not let Israel go" (Ex 5:2). Pharaoh does not know the Lord. This is the problem God will remedy through Israel's exodus from Egypt. God will "get glory over Pharaoh and all his host, *and the Egyptians shall know that I am the LORD*" (Ex 14:4, 17-18). This purpose extends beyond just Pharaoh and Egypt. God has the whole earth in view. To Pharaoh, God says, "But for this purpose I have raised you up, to show you my power, so that my name may be proclaimed in all the earth" (Ex 9:16).

We see this very thing begin to be fulfilled in the book of Joshua, when the spies enter Canaan and come to the house of Rahab the prostitute. She tells them, "I know that the LORD has given you the land, and that the fear of you has fallen upon us. . . . For we have heard how the LORD dried up the water of the Red Sea before you when you came out of Egypt . . . for the LORD your God, he is God in the heavens above and on earth beneath" (Josh 2:9-11). God is in fact becoming known among the nations through his acts of judgment on Egypt and through his mercy toward Israel. As a result, Rahab becomes a part of the people of Israel and, astonishingly, part of the lineage of Jesus, the Messiah (Mt 1:5).

J. Richard Middleton affirms that "the exodus is not just for Israel's sake (though it surely is for that), but for the sake of the wider world."[10] This dual purpose—Israel knowing the Lord *for the sake of the whole world*—becomes explicit in God's initial words to them at Mount Sinai.

ISRAEL'S VOCATION

In Exodus 19, Israel comes to Mount Sinai, where God declares his purpose for creating them and establishing his covenant with them: "You yourselves have seen what I did to the Egyptians, and how I bore you on eagles' wings and brought you to myself" (Ex 19:4). Through the exodus, God brought Israel to himself in order to have a special relationship with them. Now God has a special vocation for them: "Now therefore, if you will indeed obey my voice and keep my covenant, *you shall be my treasured possession among all peoples, for all the earth is mine; and you shall be to me a kingdom of priests and a holy nation*" (Ex 19:5-6). These titles—treasured possession, kingdom of priests, and holy nation—are rich in significance and communicate the relational, vocational, and ethical aspects of the calling God gave to humanity in creation, and that he now gives to Israel.

---

[10]J. Richard Middleton, "The Blessing of Abraham and the *Missio Dei*: Reframing the Purpose of Israel's Election in Genesis 12:1-3," in *Orthodoxy and Orthopraxis: Essays in Tribute to Paul Livermore*, ed. Douglas R. Cullum and J. Richard Middleton (Eugene, OR: Pickwick, 2020), 57.

Treasured possession. First, Israel is to be God's *treasured possession* among all peoples. This speaks to the relational aspect of Israel's glory. Israel is to be a people belonging specially to God. When Moses later explains why God chose Israel to be his treasured possession, he highlights the love from God that this title communicates: "The LORD your God has chosen you to be a people for *his treasured possession,* out of all the peoples who are on the face of the earth. It was not because you were more in number than any other people that *the LORD set his love on you* and chose you, for you were the fewest of all peoples, but *it is because the LORD loves you*" (Deut 7:6-8). As God's treasured possession, Israel is specially and uniquely loved by God. They have privileged access to God in a way that is distinct from other peoples of the earth. But the titles that follow further explain Israel's calling as God's treasured possession and show that God chose Israel to be his treasured possession from among all the peoples of the earth *for the sake of all the earth.*

Kingdom of priests. To be God's "treasured possession" carries a sense of representative responsibility, as usage throughout the ancient world shows.[11] This responsibility is further emphasized in Israel's calling to be a *kingdom of priests,* which highlights the vocational aspect of Israel's glory. Two important ideas are joined together in the phrase "kingdom of priests." First, Israel is to be a *kingdom*—a people who live under God's good rule and reign, and who themselves are given royal status. Through Israel, God will restore the kind of dominion he intended for humans at creation (Gen 1:26, 28).

Second, Israel is to be a kingdom *of priests.* Israel's priests devoted themselves to the worship of God and had special access to his presence, in which they represented the people before the Lord. They also represented the Lord to the people. By calling the nation of Israel a "kingdom of priests," God is saying that the entire nation of Israel is meant to function in this priestly role—first by being devoted to and enthralled by Yahweh, and then by representing him to the nations of the world.

Bible teacher and minister Ross Blackburn helpfully explains what this priestly role to the nations entails and in the process makes an important observation. In Exodus, the word *glory* (*kābôd*) is used exclusively in relation

---

[11]See Carmen Joy Imes, *Bearing God's Name: Why Sinai Still Matters* (Downers Grove, IL: IVP Academic, 2019), 31.

to the Lord, with one exception: the instructions for the high priest's garments, which God tells Moses are "for glory and for beauty" (Ex 28:2, 40). Blackburn comments, "In wearing the garments, Aaron effectively represented the Lord as he displayed his glory."[12] The priestly garments serve as a picture of Israel's role to the nations. As the high priest represented the Lord to Israel, now Israel, as a kingdom of priests, is to represent the Lord to the nations, displaying his glory and beauty to them. Israel is also to represent the nations before God, interceding on their behalf and directing the nations toward a true worship of the living God, serving as "a vehicle for bringing the nations to the divine presence and rule."[13]

Because Israel is a kingdom *of priests*, the nature of their kingdom is to be entirely different from the kingdoms of the world after the fall. As Stephen Dempster notes, a kingdom marked by priesthood is characterized by service of God on behalf of people and service of people on behalf of God.[14] This means they will be "a servant nation instead of a ruling nation," a people marked by self-giving love.[15]

I am reminded of a time when some of my kids wanted to play a game in which we pretended we were in a kingdom. One of them immediately said, "I want to be king!" "Why do you want to be king?" I asked. "Because then I get to do whatever I want, and I get to tell everyone else what to do!" It was a humorous (and revealing) moment. That is the way of kingship according to the world. But it's not the way of kingship for God's people. Israel is to exercise dominion by caring for one another and for God's creation, reflecting the goodness of God's rule and reign to the world, just as God intended for humans from the beginning. Dempster helpfully explains, "Israel will thus redefine the meaning of dominion—service. This will be its distinctive task, its distinguishing characteristic among the world of the nations. It will reclaim the lost dominion of humanity."[16] As God's treasured possession, Israel has the privilege of knowing God and beholding his glory.

[12]W. Ross Blackburn, *The God Who Makes Himself Known: The Missionary Heart of the Book of Exodus*, New Studies in Biblical Theology 28 (Downers Grove, IL: IVP Academic, 2012), 91.

[13]Gentry and Wellum, *Kingdom Through Covenant*, 360.

[14]Dempster, *Dominion and Dynasty*, 101.

[15]John I. Durham, *Exodus*, Word Biblical Commentary (Waco, TX: Word, 1987), 263.

[16]Dempster, *Dominion and Dynasty*, 102.

Then, as a kingdom of priests, Israel is called to mediate that glory to a watching world.

Holy nation. Finally, God calls Israel to be *a holy nation*. This speaks especially to the ethical aspect of Israel's glory. The people of Israel are to reflect God's holiness: "You shall be holy, for I the LORD your God am holy" (Lev 19:2). They are to represent God, embodying his character in themselves.

Humans, created as God's image, were to represent God in the way they exercised dominion over creation and in their relationships with one another. Now Israel is to carry this calling forward, helping to repair and restore what has been broken. As a kingdom of priests and a holy nation, they are to represent God and reflect his glory to the world, so that all peoples might come to know, love, and worship God, and so all the earth might be brought into the goodness of life under God's rule and reign.

Israel can fulfill her vocation only by remaining in relationship with God: "*If you will indeed obey my voice and keep my covenant*, you will be my treasured possession among all the peoples" (Ex 19:5). As with Adam in the Garden of Eden, so too with Israel. Trust and obedience are necessary to live in the kind of relationship with God that will enable his people to reflect his glory to the world.

CONCLUSION: NEW ADAM, SAME PURPOSE

The covenant God makes with Israel at Sinai begins with God expressing the special status he has bestowed on Israel and also the way this status is meant to bring God's blessing to all the earth. This is what God intended for humanity from the beginning (Gen 1:28) and what he reaffirmed to Abraham and his offspring (Gen 12:1-3; 22:17-18). Israel is a new Adam with the same purpose as the first Adam—indeed, God's original purpose for all of humanity. God intends to reveal his glory *to* Israel so he can reveal his glory *through* Israel.

Chapter Four

GLORY TO AND THROUGH ISRAEL, PART TWO

They exchanged the glory of God
for the image of an ox that eats grass.
They forgot God, their Savior,
who had done great things in Egypt.

PSALM 106:20-21

WHEN ISRAEL CAME TO MOUNT SINAI following the exodus from Egypt, it was like coming to a new mountain sanctuary, a new Eden. This mountain, where God had previously revealed himself to Moses in a burning bush, now becomes the focal point of God's presence and glory as he prepares to enter into covenant with his people.

But things have changed since God's people lived in their garden home, where they walked with God and had access to his glory and presence. God's glory is a terrifying thing for the people of Israel. When God appears at Mount Sinai, there are "thunders and lightnings and a thick cloud on the mountain and a very loud trumpet blast" (Ex 19:16). The mountain "was wrapped in smoke because the LORD had descended on it in fire . . . and the whole mountain trembled greatly" (Ex 19:18). In the presence of such glory, the author tells us that "all the people in the camp trembled" (Ex 19:16), and again that "the people were afraid and trembled, and they stood far off" (Ex 20:18). The response of the people of Israel is not so different from the first human couple, who, after eating from the tree of the knowledge of good and evil, were afraid and hid themselves from the face of the Lord (Gen 3:8, 10). At Sinai, the Lord shows Israel "his glory and greatness" (Deut 5:24), and the people are rightly afraid.

Sin has disrupted the relationship God's people have with him. Because we have been corrupted by sin, God's glory imposes fear, terror, and even danger to people. But God has come to this mountain to forge a new relationship with his people, to restore something of what he desired and intended when he first created humans in his image to see and to share in his glory.

In the last chapter we saw how, through the exodus from Egypt, God brought the people of Israel to himself in order to be his treasured possession, so that they might serve as a kingdom of priests and a holy nation, representing and reflecting him to all nations of the earth (Ex 19:5-6). In this chapter, we will continue our journey through the exodus to see how Israel is meant to fulfill their vocation, how they break covenant with the Lord and fail in their relationship and vocation, and, of course, how God reveals his glory in response.

GLORY THROUGH TORAH AND TABERNACLE

Exodus 19:5 provides important insight into *how* Israel is to reflect God's glory to the nations: "*If you will indeed obey my voice and keep my covenant, you shall be my treasured possession among all peoples.*" Obedience always flows from trust, as we saw in the Garden of Eden and as the Bible shows throughout Israel's history. Through trust and obedience, the people of Israel are able to live in covenant relationship with God and represent him in the earth.

There are two aspects of the covenant that become central to Israel's life as a nation: Torah and tabernacle. Each of these is given as a gift to Israel so that God might reveal his glory to and through his people.

Glory through Torah. The Hebrew word *tôrâ* means "instruction, teaching, or law." It is used to designate the first five books of the Bible. These are the instructions or laws God gave to Moses for the people of Israel. Of course, this portion of Scripture contains more than just laws. The narratives that are so foundational for understanding God and the world—creation, the fall, the exodus from Egypt, and many others—are contained in the Torah. But there are laws as well, 613 of them to be exact. Exodus 20–23 consists almost entirely of laws God gave to Moses on Mount Sinai for the people of Israel. God gives these laws to guide them in how they are to live as his covenant people, his treasured possession with a unique calling to represent God to all the nations of the earth.

I often ask my students, "Why did God give Israel the laws that he gave them?" I want them to think about the basis for the Ten Commandments, as well as the hundreds of other laws contained in the Torah. I have my students imagine with me God's heavenly courts, where God is in deliberation. How is he going to rule over his people? At this point, our exercise of imagination becomes facetious. God says, "Well, we created a nation, so now we need some laws to govern these people. What about murder? Should we make murder okay or not okay?" God flips a coin. Tails. Murder is not okay. "What about loving your neighbor?" Heads. Love will be allowed in God's kingdom. Adultery? Lying? Caring for the poor? Tails, tails, heads.

Such a scene is ridiculous. And that's the point. We know God did not arbitrarily determine laws for his people. So why did he give them the laws he did? What is the basis for his statutes and decrees in the Torah? In his excellent article "The Law of Moses and the Christian: A Compromise," David Dorsey writes, "A law reflects the mind, the personality, the priorities, the values, the likes and dislikes of the lawgiver. Each law issued by God to ancient Israel . . . reflects God's mind and ways and is therefore a theological treasure."[1]

God's laws are rooted in his character and nature. God is love, which is why the whole law can be summed up as directing people toward love for God and love for their neighbor (Mt 22:37-40; Lk 10:25-28; Rom 13:8-10). God is merciful and compassionate, and so the laws he gives direct his people toward acts of mercy and compassion. God is just, so his people are to be just and righteous in their dealings with one another. God is faithful and

---

[1]David A. Dorsey, "The Law of Moses and the Christian: A Compromise," *Journal of the Evangelical Theological Society* 34, no. 1 (September 1991): 332.

trustworthy, so all forms of faithlessness and dishonesty, including lying, bearing false witness, and adultery, are forbidden.

Through keeping his laws, Israel is to imitate God. We see this, for example, in the Sabbath command. God commands Israel to keep Sabbath because that is what God did at creation, setting a pattern for his people to follow: "For in six days the LORD made the heavens and the earth, the sea, and all that is in them, and rested on the seventh day" (Ex 20:11). Israel is to reflect God's compassion in very practical ways, such as returning a coat that is taken in pledge before nightfall, "for I am compassionate" (Ex 22:27). "In her obedience to the Law," Blackburn says, "Israel would conform to the character of the Lord. As the Lord is, so he calls his people to be."[2]

God's laws reveal what God is like, enabling his people to see his glory. And as Israel lives in accordance with God's laws, they will display his glory, reflecting God's character and nature in their lives. Israel, as God's firstborn son (Ex 4:22-23) and as a kingdom of priests (Ex 19:3-6), is meant to "display to the rest of the world within its covenant community the kind of relationships, first to God and then to one another and to the physical world, that God intended originally for all of humanity."[3] Gentry and Wellum explain,

> The only functional routes for commerce and travel between the great superpowers of the ancient world go through the tiny country given to Abram. . . . All the communication, commerce, and trade back and forth between Egypt and Mesopotamia will pass through Canaan. And when it does, what are the travelers and traders supposed to see? They are supposed to witness a group of people who demonstrate a right relationship to the one and only true God, a human way of treating each other, and a proper stewardship of the earth's resources.[4]

In other words, they should see a people who, through keeping Torah, represent God and show his glory.

---

[2]W. Ross Blackburn, *The God Who Makes Himself Known: The Missionary Heart of the Book of Exodus*, New Studies in Biblical Theology 28 (Downers Grove, IL: IVP Academic, 2012), 71.

[3]Peter J. Gentry and Stephen J. Wellum, *Kingdom Through Covenant: A Biblical-Theological Understanding of the Covenants*, 2nd ed. (Wheaton, IL: Crossway, 2018), 341.

[4]Gentry and Wellum, *Kingdom Through Covenant*, 297-98.

The second commandment—"You shall not take the name of the LORD your God in vain" (Ex 20:7)—reflects this calling for the people of Israel.[5] Old Testament scholar Carmen Imes argues convincingly that the word *take* in our English translations (from the Hebrew verb *nāsā᾽*) is better translated "bear" or "carry": "You shall not *bear* the name of the LORD your God in vain." To bear God's name does not refer directly to our speech in the way many tend to think of this command, as though it were mainly forbidding the use of God's name as a curse word. Rather, to bear or carry God's name is to represent God, living in a way that reflects his name and his character. The high priest, who served as God's chief representative, was to "bear [*nāsā᾽*] the names of the sons of Israel" on his priestly garments (Ex 28:29), representing the people before the Lord. And he was to bear the Lord's name on his forehead (Ex 28:36-38), indicating that he represented God to the people. In the same way, God calls his people, who are "a kingdom of priests" (Ex 19:6), to "bear his name," representing him well before the peoples of the earth.[6] Thus, to "bear the LORD's name in vain" is to represent him poorly, failing to live in a way that displays his character and reflects his glory.

Imes insightfully observes that the Ten Commandments "begin with the two weightiest commands—the ones that set the stage for all the others. Stated positively, they say: 1. *Worship only Yahweh.* 2. *Represent him well.*"[7] This is how Israel is to reflect God's glory. First, by beholding God's glory, revealed in the Torah. And second, by responding in love, worship, trust, and obedience, living in accordance with Torah and thereby reflecting God's glory in all the earth. "If anything," Imes says, "we learn in Exodus 20 that the law is not an end in itself. It is Israel's means of knowing Yahweh, and of living out their vocation in the world."[8]

Glory through tabernacle. A second central feature of life in Israel is the tabernacle (and later the temple). The tabernacle was an elaborate, portable tent located at the center of Israel's camp during their journey through the

---

[5]There is some debate about whether this is in fact the second or third commandment. For a helpful rationale for seeing it as the second commandment, see Carmen Joy Imes, *Bearing God's Name: Why Sinai Still Matters* (Downers Grove, IL: IVP Academic, 2019), 45-48.

[6]Imes, *Bearing God's Name*, 49-51.

[7]Imes, *Bearing God's Name*, 52.

[8]Imes, *Bearing God's Name*, 57.

wilderness on the way to the Promised Land. If you read straight through Exodus, you realize there is a lot of space devoted to the tabernacle. Exodus 25–31 consists entirely of detailed instructions the Lord gives to Moses for building the tabernacle and all its furnishings. Then Exodus 35–40 gives a play-by-play of the workmen in Israel building the tabernacle, carrying out the instructions from Exodus 25–31, with all the details from those earlier chapters repeated. It raises an important question: Why is so much attention devoted to the tabernacle? Much of the meaning and significance is easily lost on us, but it is hard to avoid the impression that, as foreign as it might seem, this must be important.

God does not leave us guessing as to why Israel is to build the tabernacle. He says, "And let them make me a sanctuary, that I may dwell in their midst" (Ex 25:8). God's desire is to live with his people. That is the tabernacle's purpose. In Exodus 29, he says more: "I will dwell among the people of Israel and will be their God. And they shall know that I am the LORD their God, who brought them out of the land of Egypt *that I might dwell among them*. I am the LORD their God" (Ex 29:45-46). The sacrificial system of the tabernacle allows Israel to live in God's presence without being consumed by his presence. And this, the Lord says, is the reason he delivered Israel from Egypt in the first place, "that I might dwell among them."

We saw in Genesis that this was God's purpose in creation. The Garden of Eden was a sanctuary where God dwelled among his people. In the garden, Adam and Eve had fellowship with God and had access to his presence and glory. Now with Israel, God again intends to dwell with his people, and the tabernacle makes this possible. In fact, just as Israel is like a new, corporate Adam, the tabernacle is like a new, portable Eden, a sanctuary for God's presence and glory to reside among his people.

When we understand this connection between the tabernacle and the sanctuary in Eden, some of the details begin to make sense:

1. The entrance to Eden faced east and, after the fall, was guarded by cherubim (Gen 3:24). Likewise, the entrance to the tabernacle was from the east, and the holy of holies was separated by a veil that had cherubim woven into it, symbolically guarding the place of God's presence (Ex 26:31-33; 38:13).

2. Gold and precious stones are closely connected to both Eden and the tabernacle. Especially interesting is the mention of onyx in Genesis 2:12, which is almost entirely associated with the tabernacle or temple in later Scripture (see Ex 25:7; 28:9, 20; 35:9, 27; 39:6, 13; 1 Chron 29:2).[9]

3. As I mentioned in chapter two, the biblical authors use the same verb for God *walking* in the garden (Gen 3:8) and *walking* in the tabernacle (Lev 26:12; Deut 23:14; 2 Sam 7:6-7).

4. I also noted the connection between Adam's role "to work . . . and keep" the garden (Gen 2:15) and the Levites' role with regard to the tabernacle, where the same two verbs (ʿābad, "work, serve"; šāmar, "keep, guard") are used together (Num 3:5-10; 8:26; 18:4-6).

5. The tabernacle is adorned with garden imagery. The golden lampstand, for example, is shaped like a tree with branches covered in almond blossoms (Ex 25:31-40), recalling the trees that filled the Garden of Eden and perhaps representing the tree of life (Gen 2:9).[10]

Additionally, God gives instructions for the sanctuary in seven stages or decrees, likely intended to recall the seven days of creation (Ex 25:1; 30:11, 17, 22, 34; 31:1, 12).[11] The sixth of these is the appointment of two individuals who are filled with the Spirit of God to make the structure of the tabernacle (Ex 31:1-6), reminiscent of the creation of humans on the sixth day and also calling to mind the two particular humans who are placed in the garden sanctuary (Gen 1:26-27; 2:7, 22). The seventh decree is about the Sabbath, just as the seventh day of creation was the day on which God rested, establishing the pattern for the Sabbath among his people (Gen 2:2-3; Ex 31:12-17).[12]

In these and other ways, the author seems to stress the point that the tabernacle is "a microcosm of the creation of the world, and its innermost

---

[9]The one exception to this is Job 28:16. Ezek 28:13 also refers to onyx, where it is again connected to the Garden of Eden.

[10]Solomon's temple contains further elaborate garden imagery. See 1 Kings 6:18, 29, 32; 7:18-20, 22, 24-26, 42, 49.

[11]Each stage begins with the phrase, "The LORD said to Moses."

[12]There are also several phrases at the end of the tabernacle's construction that seem designed to recall phrases from the completion of creation, including Ex 39:43 (Gen 1:31); Ex 39:32 (Gen 2:1); Ex 40:33 (Gen 2:2); and Ex 39:43 (Gen 2:3).

sanctuary a Garden of Eden."[13] Its purpose is to point back to the garden and
to God's original intention for humanity. At the same time, it points forward
to the fulfillment of God's plan for Eden, which was for God's people to
multiply and spread outward from Eden, filling all creation with the glory of
God and causing the whole earth to become God's sanctuary.

Through the tabernacle and its sacrificial system, God makes fellowship
between a holy God and sinful people possible once more. God is restoring
Israel to relationship with himself, the kind of relationship he intended for
humanity in creation. Through the tabernacle, his glory will dwell among
them (see Ex 40:34), and through them he plans to make his glory known
throughout the earth.

God gives tabernacle and Torah as gifts, so the people of Israel might
behold his glory, be shaped by his glory, and reflect his glory in all the earth. In
Deuteronomy, Moses prepares a new generation of Israelites to go into the
Promised Land and possess it. He reminds them of God's good laws and of
their vocation in the world given to them at Sinai, calling them to obedience
with these words:

> See, I have taught you statutes and rules, as the LORD my God commanded
> me, that you should do them in the land that you are entering to take pos-
> session of it. Keep them and do them, for that will be your wisdom and your
> understanding in the sight of the peoples, who, when they hear all these statutes,
> will say, "Surely this great nation is a wise and understanding people." *For what
> great nation is there that has a god so near to it as the LORD our God is to us,
> whenever we call upon him? And what great nation is there, that has statutes
> and rules so righteous as all this law that I set before you today?* (Deut 4:5-8)

What other nation has a god so near? What other nation has laws so just?
Tabernacle and Torah. As Israel lives with wisdom and understanding in the
sight of the peoples (Deut 4:6), the nations will see a people who embody
what humans were meant to be from the very beginning—those who know
God and behold his glory and who reflect God and show his glory. God reveals
his glory to Israel so that he can reveal his glory through Israel.

---

[13]Stephen Dempster, *Dominion and Dynasty: A Biblical Theology of the Hebrew Bible*, New Studies
in Biblical Theology (Downers Grove, IL: IVP Academic, 2003), 102.

ISRAEL'S FALL

We don't go far in Israel's history before their story, like Adam's before them, takes a tragic turn. In a breathtaking scene in Exodus 24, Moses, Aaron and his sons, and the seventy elders of Israel go up on Mount Sinai, "and they saw the God of Israel. There was under his feet as it were a pavement of sapphire stone, like the very heaven for clearness. And he did not lay his hand on the chief men of the people of Israel; they beheld God, and ate and drank" (Ex 24:10-11).

Later Jewish tradition refers to this event as a wedding feast. God and his people have joined themselves in covenant, and now they sit down to eat and drink together. The phrase "they beheld God" is easy to rush past, but it is stunning in its significance. This is the very thing for which God created people. And now on Sinai, Israel's representative leaders get to behold their God and eat a meal with him. It's an incredible moment of mercy and grace in Israel's story. It's a moment much like the end of Genesis 2 in the Garden of Eden, where you can almost feel the richness and goodness and joy.

The very next time we encounter Aaron and the people of Israel, though, the transition is as stark as the one that happens between Genesis 2–3. After the feast, God calls Moses to come up further on the mountain and to enter the cloud, where "the appearance of the glory of the LORD was like a devouring fire on the top of the mountain in the sight of the people of Israel" (Ex 24:17). While Moses is on the mountain receiving instructions for the tabernacle, the people of Israel grow weary of waiting for him to return. They gather together, approach Aaron, and say, "Up, make us gods who shall go before us. As for this Moses, the man who brought us up out of the land of Egypt, we do not know what has become of him" (Ex 32:1). Like a bride who commits adultery on her honeymoon, Israel has barely begun their covenant relationship with the Lord before they break the first commandment (Ex 20:3-6) by turning to idolatry. When the psalmist reflects back on this moment, he captures Israel's actions with these words:

> They made a calf in Horeb
>   and worshiped a metal image.
> *They exchanged the glory of God*
>   for the image of an ox that eats grass. (Ps 106:19-20)

Israel traded the most precious thing imaginable—God's glory—for a metal calf, and said, "These are your gods, O Israel, who brought you up out of the land of Egypt!" (Ex 32:4). Aaron built an altar to the calf, the people offered burnt offerings in worship, and the beautiful wedding banquet in the Lord's presence now gives way to an idolatrous feast: "And the people sat down to eat and drink and rose up to play" (Ex 32:6).

In Exodus 32, we witness Israel's fall. The prophet Hosea, generations later, laments, "But *like Adam* they transgressed the covenant; there they dealt faithlessly with me" (Hos 6:7). Like Adam before her, Israel now turns away from the Lord and exchanges God's glory for a lie, worshiping and serving the creature rather than the Creator (Rom 1:25).[14]

WHY MOSES ASKS GOD TO "SHOW ME YOUR GLORY"

Now, after journeying through the exodus from Egypt and Israel's covenant with God at Mount Sinai, we come to the point in the narrative that we began with in the last chapter—Moses' request to see God's glory.

In response to Israel's sin, God tells Moses he is going to destroy Israel and make a great nation of Moses. But Moses intercedes on behalf of the people, appealing to the Lord's reputation among the nations: "Why should the Egyptians say, 'With evil intent did he bring them out, to kill them in the mountains and to consume them from the face of the earth'?" (Ex 32:12). Moses also appeals to God's promises to Abraham, Isaac, and Jacob (Ex 32:13). In another act of astonishing mercy, the Lord responds to Moses' intercession and "relented from the disaster that he had spoken of bringing on his people" (Ex 32:14).

God will not wipe out the people of Israel as they deserve. But he tells Moses that he will not go up with Israel to the land he promised to give to them: "I will send an angel before you, and I will drive out the Canaanites, the Amorites, the Hittites, the Perizzites, the Hivites, and the Jebusites. Go up to a land flowing with milk and honey; but I will not go up among you, lest I consume you on the way, for you are a stiff-necked people" (Ex 33:2-3).

---

[14]In Rom 1:23-25, Paul links the fall in Gen 3 and the fall in Ex 32, showing how Adam and Israel's stories are actually the same story—the story of all humanity living in sin and rebellion against God. The association of the golden calf with the fall of Adam is also common in Jewish rabbinic literature.

When Moses reports this to the people of Israel, they recognize it for what it is: a "disastrous word" (Ex 33:4). God's presence is what makes Israel distinct among all people on the face of the earth (Ex 33:16). As we saw in Exodus 19:5-6, God brought Israel to himself so they might be his treasured possession among all peoples and so they might reflect his glory through the earth. For God to leave them, removing their access to his presence and glory, is indeed disastrous. It renders both their relationship with God (seeing his glory) and their calling to the nations (showing his glory) impossible. To their credit, the people do not want God's gifts without God himself: "When the people heard this disastrous word, they mourned, and no one put on his ornaments" (Ex 33:4).

Moses again intercedes for the people of Israel, pleading for God's presence to go with them: "If your presence will not go with me, do not bring us up from here. For how shall it be known that I have found favor in your sight, I and your people? Is it not in your going with us, so that we are distinct, I and your people, from every other people on the face of the earth?" (Ex 33:15-16). As we have come to expect, the Lord consents to Moses' plea: "And the LORD said to Moses, 'This very thing that you have spoken I will do, for you have found favor in my sight, and I know you by name'" (Ex 33:17).

God's response elicits one more request: "Moses said, 'Please show me your glory'" (Ex 33:18). It's as if God's promise to go with his people allows Moses to let out the collective breath being held by Israel. When God promises to go with them so that his glory will be among them, it seems the words almost tumble out of Moses' mouth in a mixture of both relief and longing: "Please show me your glory."

Amazingly, God says yes. At the invitation of God, Moses once more ascends Mount Sinai, and God causes his glory to pass by Moses (Ex 34:6-7). He reveals to Moses the glory of his mercy and grace, the glory of his love and forgiveness, and the glory of his justice.

Moses, undone in the presence of God's glory, "quickly bowed his head toward the earth and worshiped" (Ex 34:8). Emboldened by the revelation of God's glory to him, Moses once more requests that God go with Israel and that he forgive their sin and take them for his inheritance (Ex 34:9). The Lord, in demonstration of the glory of his mercy, steadfast love, and forgiveness that he has just shown to Moses, reestablishes his covenant with Israel: "And he said, 'Behold, I am making a covenant. Before all your people I will do marvels, such as have not been created in all the earth or in any nation. And *all the people among whom you are shall see the work of the LORD*, for it is an awesome thing that I will do with you'" (Ex 34:10).

God shows special love to the people of Israel, restoring their relationship with him. When he does, he has the nations of the earth in view: "All the people among whom you are shall see the work of the LORD." God's glory to his people and God's glory through his people. This is the current that runs beneath all God does in creation and redemption and all he does in his acts toward Israel.

MOSES' GLORY

So brilliant is this display of God's glory to Moses that when he comes down from the mountain, the people see God's glory radiating from him: "The skin of his face shone" (Ex 34:29). In Moses we see a living portrait of God's purpose for his people, whom he created to behold his glory and to reflect his glory to others and to the world.

Though Moses was unaware that his face was shining, Aaron and the people saw his face, "and they were afraid to come near him" (Ex 34:30). Moses has become a mediator of God's glory to the people of Israel. But as we have seen many times now, in a sinful state, God's people cannot look directly on his face or behold his glory. So Moses "put a veil over his face" (Ex 34:33), shielding the Israelites from a direct encounter with God's glory that they were not able to bear.[15]

The priests of Israel would later bless the people with words that seem to have their origin in this experience of Moses: "The LORD bless you and keep you; *the LORD make his face to shine upon you* and be gracious to you; *the LORD lift up his countenance upon you* and give you peace" (Num 6:24-26).

---

[15]Scott Hafemann, *Paul, Moses, and the History of Israel: The Letter/Spirit Contrast and the Argument from Scripture in 2 Corinthians 3* (Peabody, MA: Hendrickson, 1996), 223, explains that the veil functions in the same way as the fence around the bottom of Sinai in Ex 19:12 and the curtain before the holy of holies in the tabernacle "that both separates and protects people from the glory of God." Likewise, the cloud in the book of Exodus serves the same purpose (see, e.g., Ex 13:21-22; 16:10; 19:9, 16; 24:16; 33:9-10; 34:5; 40:34-35).

Of this blessing that the priests are to speak over the people, the Lord says, "So shall they put my name upon the people of Israel, and I will bless them" (Num 6:27). God's name—his character, his glory—is to be imprinted on his people as he makes his face to shine on them, as he lifts up his countenance on them. This was Moses' experience. And it is meant to be the experience of all God's people. The apostle Paul, following an extended reflection on the events of Exodus 34, declares to Christians at Corinth, "And we all, with unveiled face, beholding the glory of the Lord, are being transformed into the same image from one degree of glory to another" (2 Cor 3:18).

Paul shows that "the Lord" is Christ, who removes the veil and enables access to God's glory in an ultimate sense (2 Cor 3:16). As we behold "the glory of God in the face of Jesus Christ" (2 Cor 4:6), we are transformed into the same image—the image we were meant to reflect from the very beginning (Gen 1:26). God plans to reveal his glory to his people. And he plans to reveal his glory through his people. From Adam, to Israel, to the church, God's purpose remains the same.

GLORY COMES DOWN

Exodus 34 is certainly a high point in the narrative. But the climax of the story comes at the end of the book. Following the completion of the work of the tabernacle (Ex 40:33), the glory shown to Moses that caused his face to shine now descends on the sanctuary: "Then the cloud covered the tent of meeting, and the glory of the LORD filled the tabernacle. And Moses was not able to enter the tent of meeting because the cloud settled on it, and the glory of the LORD filled the tabernacle" (Ex 40:34-35).

Throughout Israel's wilderness wanderings, God's glory would continue to reside among Israel and would direct their paths. When the cloud would go up from the tabernacle, the people would set out and follow it, until the cloud would settle again and Israel would make camp (Ex 40:36-38). God's glory in the tabernacle makes Israel distinct (Ex 33:16) and is one of the means that enables them to fulfill the vocation God gave them in Exodus 19:5-6. This people dwells in God's presence. They have access to his presence and glory, even if only in a mediated way. And they are to live as a kingdom of priests and a holy nation, reflecting his glory to the world.

From this point on in Israel's history, God's glory will be associated with Israel's sanctuary. Looking ahead in Israel's history to the time when King Solomon builds the temple, which replaces the mobile tabernacle and provides a more permanent dwelling place for God, we are told that

> As soon as Solomon finished his prayer, fire came down from heaven and consumed the burnt offering and the sacrifices, and the glory of the LORD filled the temple. And the priests could not enter the house of the LORD, because the glory of the LORD filled the LORD's house. When all the people of Israel saw the fire come down and the glory of the LORD on the temple, they bowed down with their faces to the ground on the pavement and worshiped and gave thanks to the LORD, saying, "For he is good, for his steadfast love endures forever." (2 Chron 7:1-3)

Like Moses' response to the revelation of God's glory on Sinai (Ex 34:8), the people respond to the revelation of God's glory in the temple by bowing with their faces to the ground and worshiping. But the similarities between these two events go further. The words they speak recall the revelation of God's glory to Moses on Mount Sinai: "For he is good, for his steadfast love endures forever" (2 Chron 7:3).

The sanctuary in Israel is the place on earth where God's glory dwells among his people, and it stands as a reminder that God is good, God is merciful, and God is just. Ultimately, God's dwelling place in Israel serves God's larger purpose of granting all people access to God. Solomon prays that as the nations of the earth come and pray toward the temple, God would answer their prayers, so that "all the peoples of the earth may know your name and fear you" (2 Chron 6:33). "All the peoples of the earth" is never far from view in God's dealings with his people. God reveals his glory to his people, so that God can reveal his glory through his people, so that God's glory can fill all the earth.

We have seen that the tabernacle is a microcosm of creation, pointing back to Eden and to God's original intention for his world. And it also points forward, a visible symbol of God's plan and purpose for all creation. Exodus 40 anticipates what God will do with all creation, as he restores creation and fills it with his glory just as his glory fills the tabernacle.[16]

---

[16]L. Michael Morales, *Who Shall Ascend the Mountain of the Lord: A Biblical Theology of the Book of Leviticus*, New Studies in Biblical Theology 37 (Downers Grove, IL: IVP Academic, 2015), 117.

SEPARATION REMAINS

Even as we look forward to where the story is heading, we are reminded of the problem of sin. When God's glory fills the tabernacle, not even Moses is able to enter (Ex 40:35). This is reminiscent of God's words to Moses in Exodus 33:20, "You cannot see my face, for man shall not see me and live." It reminds us of the problem introduced in the Garden of Eden: we were made for God's glory, but in our sinful state we cannot bear it.

The book of Leviticus will have much to say about how this problem is resolved in the short term, as the sacrificial system is gifted to Israel and priests become mediators of God's presence and glory to his people. But for the full resolution in the biblical story, we must wait until the coming of the Messiah, when the word becomes flesh and dwells (or "tabernacles") among us, revealing God's glory and restoring the fellowship God intends to have with his people (Jn 1:14-18).

ADAM'S STORY ON REPEAT

When we peek ahead into Israel's future, we find the nation of Israel living Adam's story on repeat. During the conquest of the land of Canaan, the time of the judges, and the history of Israel's kings, the story is the same. Time and again Israel breaks covenant with the Lord. They do not trust him, so they do not obey him. They do not respond rightly to the revelation of his glory. And they do not represent him well among the nations.

There's an important moment in Israel's history in Numbers 13–14, an incident that in many ways parallels the golden calf incident in Exodus 32 and provides its counterpart. When Moses later recounts all of Israel's rebellion, he highlights these two episodes, as though they are bookends to her young history and sum up the ongoing state of the people's hearts (see Deut 9:1-21, 23-29).

Israel has come up to the edge of the Promised Land. They send spies into the land to bring back a report. And when the spies return, they cause the people's hearts to melt with fear. Israel rebels against the Lord, refusing to enter the Promised Land, choosing instead to return to Egypt. This is another tragic fall.

In response to the people's distrust and disobedience, "the glory of the LORD appeared at the tent of meeting to all the people of Israel" (Num 14:10).

In a scene reminiscent of Exodus 32, the Lord tells Moses he will destroy the people and make a new nation from Moses (Num 14:11-12). Again Moses intercedes for the people. He appeals to God's reputation among the nations (Num 14:13-16) and also to the revelation of God's glory given to him following the golden calf incident:

> And now, please let the power of the Lord be great as you have promised, saying, "The Lord is slow to anger and abounding in steadfast love, forgiving iniquity and transgression, but he will by no means clear the guilty, visiting the iniquity of the fathers on the children, to the third and the fourth generation." Please pardon the iniquity of this people, according to the greatness of your steadfast love, just as you have forgiven this people, from Egypt until now. (Num 14:17-19)

Once again, God responds favorably to Moses' intercession:

> Then the LORD said, "I have pardoned, according to your word. But truly, as I live, and as all the earth shall be filled with the glory of the LORD, none of the men who have seen my glory and my signs that I did in Egypt and in the wilderness, and yet have put me to the test these ten times and have not obeyed my voice, shall see the land that I swore to give to their fathers. And none of those who despised me shall see it." (Num 14:20-23)

A few things are noteworthy. First, God says he will pardon, but he will also judge. His response is one of mercy and justice, according to the revelation of his glory in Exodus 34:5-6, and which we saw demonstrated in his response to sin and rebellion in the early Genesis narratives.

Second, God reaffirms his purpose that he intended in creation and has not abandoned: "*All the earth shall be filled with the glory of the LORD*" (Num 14:21). This remains God's plan, though his people continually fail to trust God and partner with him in carrying it out. Still, he passionately affirms his commitment to spread his glory through all the earth.

Finally, his judgment will fall on those "who have seen my glory and my signs that I did in Egypt and in the wilderness, and yet have put me to the test these ten times and have not obeyed my voice" (Num 14:22). It is difficult to identify exactly what ten times the Lord is referring to. But the point, it seems, is that in their short history as a nation, though God has revealed his glory to Israel repeatedly, they have continually rebelled against the Lord and responded to the revelations of his glory with distrust and disobedience.

This will continue to be Israel's story: distrust, disobedience, failing to see God's glory and to respond appropriately, failing to obey God's covenant and to reflect his glory to the world. As with Adam, so with all who descend from Adam. Israel replays Adam's story again and again. And like Adam and Eve, who were banished from the garden, Israel too will finally be banished from the Promised Land, when God sends them into exile among the nations to whom they have dishonored God.

Returning to our diagram, we can depict Israel's history, as seen in Exodus and beyond, like this:

A. From his fallen world,

B. God chooses Abraham and his descendants to know him and to take up Adam's vocation. He redeems the descendants of Abraham out of Egypt

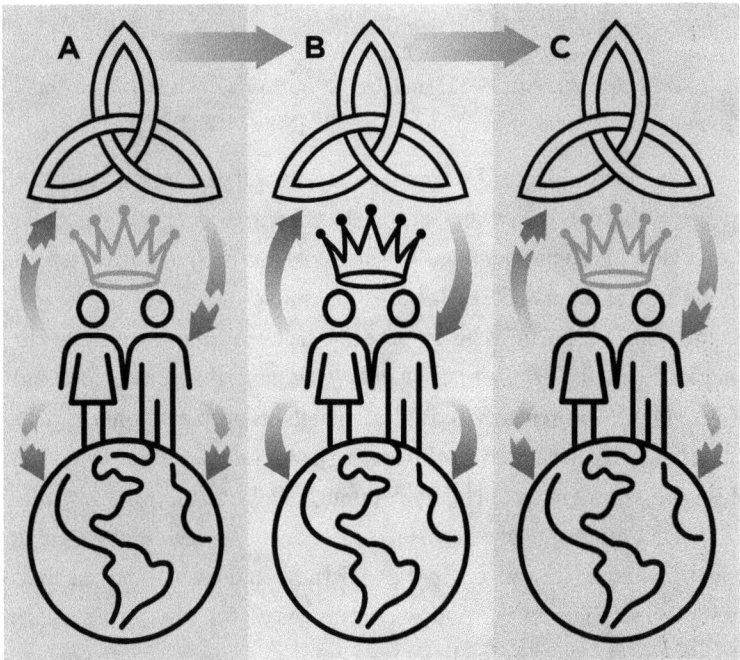

Figure 4.1. God redeems Israel / Israel (like Adam) turns from God's glory

and enters into covenant with them. The people of Israel have a special relationship with God, and he commissions them as his representatives to the world. God reveals himself to them and plans to reveal himself through them to all of creation. He gives his law to guide them in the way they relate to God, to one another, and to creation. His glory dwells among them in the tabernacle. By trust and obedience, God's people are to reflect the character and kingship of God and bring blessing to all creation.

C. But like the first humans, Israel turns from God's glory and will ultimately end up in exile, banished from the place of God's presence and glory, just like their predecessors in the Garden of Eden.

CONCLUSION: IS THERE ANY HOPE?

This, in short form, is the story of Israel that runs through the rest of the Old Testament. It is a story of God's purpose, begun in creation, continuing through Israel, and always coming to the same tragic end. In all this, God reveals his glory through mercy and judgment. In many ways, Exodus is a retelling of Adam's story, but more than that, it is the revelation, in new and greater depths, of the glory of God.

Israel's history once again leaves us with the question: Can God's glory ever be restored to his people? Can the celebration eternally enjoyed between Father, Son, and Spirit, and shared through creation, ever return to his world? And God once again provides an answer. Next it will come through his prophets, to whom we now turn our attention.

Chapter Five

ISAIAH

ALL FLESH WILL SEE THE GLORY OF THE LORD

Arise, shine, for your light has come,
and the glory of the LORD has risen upon you.
For behold, darkness shall cover the earth,
and thick darkness the peoples;
but the LORD will arise upon you,
and his glory will be seen upon you.
And nations will come to your light,
and kings to the brightness of your rising.

ISAIAH 60:1-3

THE PRINT OF A PAINTING hangs above my bedroom dresser. It is titled *Simeon's Moment*, originally painted by artist Ron DiCianni. The painting captures a moment recorded in Luke's Gospel, when the old man Simeon takes the baby Jesus up in his arms and blesses God.

Luke describes Simeon as "righteous and devout, waiting for the consolation of Israel" (Lk 2:25). *Consolation* refers to comfort after hardship and loss. We've seen how Israel's history throughout the Old Testament was a repeated enactment of Adam's sin in the garden, a downward spiral, until Israel ultimately faced judgment and exile. The people of Israel were unable to love God from the heart and live as the righteous, glorious people God created them to be. So they were banished from God's presence, carried away captive by foreign nations. By the time of Simeon, many Jews had returned to the Promised Land, but they were still living under the dominion of Rome. Simeon was waiting for God's promised consolation, the "comfort" Isaiah prophesied:[1]

> Comfort, comfort, my people, says your God. (Is 40:1)

> For the Lord comforts Zion;
>> he comforts all her waste places
> and makes her wilderness like Eden,
>> her desert like the garden of the Lord;
> joy and gladness will be found in her,
>> thanksgiving and the voice of song. (Is 51:3)

The Spirit had revealed to Simeon that he would not die until he saw the Lord's Messiah (Lk 2:26), the one who would bring the promised consolation.

Now the day has come. The Spirit leads Simeon to the temple at the same time that a young Jewish couple comes with their newborn son to present him to the Lord and to make an offering (Lk 2:27). As Simeon holds their child in his arms, all that he has hoped and longed for is coming to pass. The look on his face in the painting brilliantly captures the overwhelming joy and relief expressed in Simeon's words:

> Lord, now you are letting your servant depart in peace,
>> according to your word;
> for my eyes have seen your salvation
>> that you have prepared in the presence of all peoples,
> a light for revelation to the Gentiles,
>> and for glory to your people Israel. (Lk 2:29-32)

---

[1]In the Septuagint (the Greek translation of the Old Testament, from which the New Testament authors often quote), the word for "comfort" (paraklēsis) in Isaiah is the same word used in Lk 2:25—Simeon was "waiting for the consolation/comfort [paraklēsis] of Israel."

Simeon was living in light of God's promises of salvation. When Simeon thinks of these promises, he thinks of two things: (1) light for revelation to Gentiles (non-Israelite nations) and (2) glory to Israel. Simeon carried a hope that God's glory would be restored to and through his people, extending to all peoples of the earth. The Old Testament prophets were the fuel for this hope.

Nearly every line of Simeon's exultant declaration drips with words taken from the prophet Isaiah, who speaks of God's light going forth to the nations (Is 42:6; 49:6; 60:3) when God's glory is restored to his people (Is 60:1-2). When Simeon sees the Messiah, he is witnessing the fulfillment of God's plan and purpose implemented in creation and reiterated throughout the Old Testament: *God intends to fill the earth with his glory through a people who share in and reflect his glory.*

In this chapter, we will see how the prophet Isaiah develops the biblical theme of the glory of God and how the words and visions the Lord gives to him create an expectation of glory restored to God's people and reaching to the ends of the earth.

THE GOOD NEWS OF GOD'S REIGN

Isaiah has sometimes been called "the Fifth Gospel"—Matthew, Mark, Luke, John, *and Isaiah*. The book of Isaiah proclaims the gospel (or good news) that God is going to come as king to reclaim his people and his world, and he will do this through his Messiah, the promised king from David's line whose dominion will extend to the ends of the earth. In a spectacular proclamation of this good news, Isaiah declares,

> How beautiful upon the mountains
>   are the feet of him who brings *good news,*
> who publishes peace, who brings *good news* of happiness,
>   who publishes salvation,
>   who says to Zion, *"Your God reigns."* (Is 52:7)

"Good news!" Isaiah announces. "God is taking charge again, coming to reign and set things right." Isaiah continues,

> The voice of your watchmen—they lift up their voice;
>   together they sing for joy;

for eye to eye they see
> *the return of the LORD to Zion.*
Break forth together into singing,
> you waste places of Jerusalem,
for the LORD has comforted his people;
> he has redeemed Jerusalem.
The LORD has bared his holy arm
> before the eyes of all the nations,
and all the ends of the earth shall see
> *the salvation of our God.* (Is 52:8-10)

Isaiah's good news is that God is returning to reign over his people. God first established his reign over the earth at creation. It is the reason he created, so that his dominion might spread through his world, bringing the life and joy of the triune God to his creation. Isaiah proclaimed "the return of the Lord to Zion" after years of sorrow and judgment on Israel and promised that "all the ends of the earth shall see the salvation of our God."

GLORY RETURNS TO ZION

To understand the significance of this announcement of God's return to Zion, it will be helpful to go back a bit into Israel's history. Centuries prior to Isaiah's prophecies, King David made Jerusalem (also called Zion) the capital city of Israel. A significant moment in David's reign occurred when he brought the ark of the covenant, containing the two stone tablets God gave to Moses with the Ten Commandments written on them (Ex 34:1-4), into Jerusalem to be placed in the holy of holies within the tabernacle.

The ark of the covenant was a physical representation of God's presence and glory. Prior to David's reign, God had allowed the ark to be captured by the Philistines in battle in an act of divine judgment. Eli and his sons, who were priests in Israel, died in this judgment. Eli's daughter-in-law went into labor and gave birth to a son when she heard the news that the ark had been captured and her father-in-law and husband were dead: "And she named the child Ichabod, saying, 'The glory has departed from Israel!'" (1 Sam 4:21). *Kābôd* is the Hebrew word commonly translated "glory." When you place a negation (*'î*, "not") in front of it, you have the name Ichabod, "no glory." It's a good summary of Israel's sad history.

But when David became king, he captured Jerusalem from the Jebusites and made it his capital (2 Sam 5:6-10). Then he brought the ark of the covenant into Jerusalem, back to its home in the tabernacle, where it served as an emblem of the glory of God dwelling in the midst of Israel (2 Sam 6). The event was marked with joy and celebration, singing and dancing. The Lord was coming to Zion! Zion would be like a new Garden of Eden, the epicenter of God's presence, from which God's glory was to radiate outward through his people, drawing all nations and peoples into relationship with the living God.

However, we saw in the last chapter that Israel's history was filled with unfaithfulness. Isaiah prophesies to the people of Israel at a time when, after reliving Adam's story for centuries on end, they will experience the consequences of their sin as Adam did. They will be carried by other nations out of the Promised Land and into exile—banished from the garden, so to speak—sent away from God's presence and glory. Yet even as he proclaims judgment, Isaiah tells of a future restoration that is soon to come. The people will see "the return of the LORD to Zion" (Is 52:8). There will be singing and celebration. God will come to dwell with his people and to reign as king once more. And when he does, Isaiah says, "all the ends of the earth shall see the salvation of our God" (Is 52:10).

Isaiah prophesies a new exodus, a return of God's people from exile, and a new creation in which God's people and his world will be delivered from bondage and restored to what they were always meant to be. God's glory, revealed *to* his people and *through* his people, is a significant theme in Isaiah's portrait of this great restoration that God is going to accomplish through the Messiah, his anointed king.

THE EARTH WILL BE FULL OF HIS GLORY

One of the better-known scenes in the book of Isaiah is the prophet's vision in Isaiah 6. The Lord is "sitting upon a throne, high and lifted up; and the train of his robe filled the temple" (Is 6:1). Around him are winged seraphim, calling out to one another, "Holy, holy, holy is the LORD of hosts; the whole earth is full of his glory!" (Is 6:3).

The seraphim bear witness to God's holiness. He is above and beyond all others, in a class all his own, incomparable and wonderful beyond description. They also proclaim what God has declared all through the unfolding story of the Bible: he intends to fill creation with his glory. The seraphim anticipate the fulfillment of God's plan, declaring it as if already accomplished, "The whole earth is full of his glory!"

ISRAEL'S FRUIT WILL FILL THE WHOLE WORLD

Isaiah's prophecies about what God will do in the future (namely, fill the earth with glory) are linked to the reality of Israel's present state. Much of the book recounts Israel's (and humanity's) long and painful history. God's people have not seen his glory and delighted in it. As a result, they have not spread his glory and displayed it throughout the earth.

One image Isaiah uses to convey this is of Israel as a vineyard. Rather than "being fruitful" as God intended (Gen 1:28), Israel has borne no grapes (Is 5:1-4). They have not produced the fruit of justice and righteousness (Is 5:7). So God is going to make them a desolate land, trampled down and overgrown with briars and thorns (Is 5:5-6).

However, Isaiah's words of judgment come with a corresponding hope. Isaiah 27 portrays a redeemed, fruitful Israel:

In that day,
"A pleasant vineyard, sing of it!
 I, the LORD, am its keeper;
 every moment I water it.
 Lest anyone punish it,
I keep it night and day;
 I have no wrath." . . .
In days to come Jacob shall take root,
 Israel shall blossom and put forth shoots
 and *fill the whole world with fruit*. (Is 27:2-4, 6)

This is one of the many ways Isaiah links Israel's redemption with God's original plan to fill the earth with his image and glory, as his people "fill the whole world with fruit."

This particular image is the closing scene of a prophecy that begins in Isaiah 24, where God proclaims coming judgment on Israel and on all creation: "On that day the Lord will punish the host of heaven, in heaven, and the kings of the earth, on the earth" (Is 24:21). But through God's judgment comes restoration:

> Then the moon will be confounded
>   and the sun ashamed,
> for the LORD of hosts reigns
>   on Mount Zion and in Jerusalem,
> and *his glory will be before his elders*. (Is 24:23)

Here Isaiah looks back to Exodus and the feast on Mount Sinai, when God established his covenant with Israel, and the seventy elders of Israel "beheld God, and ate and drank" (Ex 24:11). But the prophet adds a twist: "On this mountain the LORD of hosts will make for *all peoples* a feast of rich food, a feast of well-aged wine, of rich food full of marrow, of aged wine well refined" (Is 25:6). Isaiah sees a future day when God will bring about what the covenant with Israel was always aiming toward. The elders Isaiah sees include members not just of Israel but of the entire world. "All peoples" behold God's glory and feast in his presence. The result is the overturning of everything that human sin and disobedience unleashed on the world:

> And he will swallow up on this mountain
>   the covering that is cast over all peoples,
>   the veil that is spread over all nations.
>   He will swallow up death forever;
> and the LORD GOD will wipe away tears from all faces,
>   and the reproach of his people he will take away from all the earth,
> for the LORD has spoken. (Is 25:7-8)

Mount Zion becomes the place of the revelation of God's glory to the whole earth.[2] In Isaiah, Zion-Jerusalem reaches beyond a particular physical location in Israel and stands for the presence and rule of God in the whole world.[3] God plans to manifest his glory to all people, and all people are welcomed to the feast.

---

[2] Is 4:2-6 is a similar vision of God's glory covering Mount Zion, presented in images drawn from the narrative of Israel at Mount Sinai in the book of Exodus.

[3] J. Gordon McConville, *Isaiah*, Baker Commentary on the Old Testament Prophetic Books (Grand Rapids, MI: Baker Academic, 2023), 183.

The reign of death—the consequence for Adam and Eve's sin in the garden, which spread through the world—will be overturned. God will wipe all tears away. And he will remove the reproach from his people. This is what happens when the King—the Lord himself—returns to Zion and makes his glory known.

WHEN GOD COMES . . . GLORY TO ALL THE EARTH

The return of the Lord to reign and the revelation of his glory to his people are repeated and interconnected themes that run throughout Isaiah's visions. The Lord promises to come to judge and to save his people. When he does, Isaiah says, his glory will be revealed to his people, to all peoples, and to all creation.

In Isaiah 35 the prophet paints a stunning picture of a renewed, glory-filled world. The peoples of the earth will "see the glory of the LORD, the majesty of our God" (Is 35:2). The revelation of God's glory, which brings life and joy to everything (Is 35:1-2), is tied to God coming as king to judge and to save: "Behold, your God will come with vengeance, with the recompense of God. He will come and save you" (Is 35:4).

When God makes his glory and majesty known, all creation will feel the effects. The wilderness will rejoice and blossom, and dry and barren places will become springs teeming with life (Is 35:1-2, 6-7). Blind eyes will be opened, the ears of the deaf will hear, the lame man will leap like a deer, and the mute will sing for joy (Is 35:5-6).[4] God's people will walk in the way of holiness, and those ransomed by him will "come to Zion with singing; everlasting joy shall be upon their heads; they shall obtain gladness and joy, and sorrow and sighing shall flee away" (Is 35:10). Isaiah's vision of God's glory spreading and bringing life and joy is breathtaking in its scope and its beauty.

Similarly, in a key turning point in the book, Isaiah 40 proclaims Israel's consolation after receiving judgment for her sins:

Comfort, comfort my people, says your God.
Speak tenderly to Jerusalem,
    and cry to her
that her warfare is ended,
    that her iniquity is pardoned,

---

[4]This, of course, is exactly what we see in the Gospels, when Jesus (the messianic king of Isaiah's prophecies) comes and begins to restore God's rule and reign to his world.

    that she has received from the Lord's hand
        double for all her sins. (Is 40:1-2)

Restoration follows judgment, and once more this restoration centers on the revelation of God's glory, which comes to everything and everyone:

    A voice cries:
    "In the wilderness prepare the way of the Lord;
        make straight in the desert a highway for our God.
    Every valley shall be lifted up,
        and every mountain and hill be made low;
    the uneven ground shall become level,
        and the rough places a plain.
    And the glory of the Lord shall be revealed,
        and all flesh shall see it together,
        for the mouth of the Lord has spoken." (Is 40:3-5)

A day is coming when God will definitively make his glory known. All flesh will see it. And this will happen when the Lord comes to reign once more: "Behold, the Lord God comes with might, and his arm rules for him" (Is 40:10). This is Isaiah's "good news" (Is 40:9). God is returning as king, and his kingship will affect every aspect of his world.

THE SERVANT OF THE LORD

But how will the glory of the Lord be revealed to all flesh? How will God come as king and manifest his rule throughout the earth? The Servant songs of Isaiah 40–55 answer these questions.[5] They tell of God's Servant, who will establish justice for distant lands and be a light for the nations (Is 42:4, 6). He will glorify God and cause his salvation to reach to the ends of the earth (Is 49:3, 6). And he will bear the sins and griefs of his people and bring peace with God by suffering in their place (Is 53:4-5, 11-12). It becomes evident that the Servant is a representative from Israel who does for the people what they—through all their tortured history—could not do for themselves.

    The Servant songs culminate in a celebration of the Servant's work, described in Isaiah 54–55. By his suffering, the Servant will heal Israel's

---

[5]There are four Servant songs in Isaiah: Is 42:1-4; 49:1-6; 50:4-9; 52:13–53:12.

estrangement from God, and God will once more become a husband to his people (Is 54:5). Through him, God will reestablish his covenant with Israel, and he will never remove his steadfast love or his covenant of peace from them (Is 54:10). It will be "an everlasting covenant, my steadfast, sure love for David" (Is 55:3). The prophecy recalls God's promise to David that one of his sons would rule on the throne and bring peace and justice forever (see 1 Chron 17:11-14).

Isaiah has already prophesied of a child who will be born, who will sit on the throne of David, and whose reign will extend through all the world, bringing peace, justice, and righteousness (Is 9:6-7). And he has told of a coming "shoot from the stump of Jesse, and a branch from his roots [that] shall bear fruit" (Is 11:1).[6] This branch will bring universal peace to all creation: "They shall not hurt or destroy in all my holy mountain; for the earth shall be full of the knowledge of the LORD as the waters cover the sea" (Is 11:9). This is the work of the Messiah, "the root of Jesse, who shall stand as a signal for the peoples—of him shall the nations inquire, and his resting place shall be glorious" (Is 11:10).

Now, in Isaiah 40–55, it becomes clear that through God's Servant, all God's people become recipients of the steadfast love promised to David (Is 55:3). And through them the nations will be drawn to God's good rule established through the Davidic king:[7]

> Behold, you shall call a nation that you do not know,
>   and a nation that did not know you shall run to you,
> because of the LORD your God, and of the Holy One of Israel,
>   for he has glorified you. (Is 55:5)

When God glorifies his Servant, his people will share in his glory, and all nations will be drawn to them (and to the Lord) as a result. This idea becomes the dominant note Isaiah leaves us with in the final section of the book, Isaiah 56–66.

---

[6]Jesse was David's father. "A shoot from the stump of Jesse" refers to God's promise to raise up a son from David's line and to establish his throne forever (1 Chron 17:11-12).

[7]The idea of other nations coming and joining themselves to God and to his people is a common theme in Isaiah. See, e.g., Is 2:2-4; 55:5; 60:3; 66:18, 20-21.

GOD'S GLORY ON HIS PEOPLE

Isaiah 56–66 forms the closing unit of Isaiah's prophecies. These chapters proclaim the universal mission of God's people, a mission that has everything to do with God's glory. The section is structured as a chiasm, a literary technique biblical authors commonly use. Chiasms, sometimes referred to as literary sandwiches, are formed of two parts that mirror each other, with the central element being the main idea the author wishes to emphasize, the meat of the sandwich, we might say. In Isaiah 56–66, the sandwich looks like this:[8]

Foreign peoples will come to God (Is 56:1-8)

    Israel's unrighteousness and helpless condition (Is 56:9–59:15)

        God, the Divine Warrior, will rescue his people (Is 59:15-21)

           God's glory restored to his people and seen by the nations (Is 60:1–62:12)

        God, the Divine Warrior, will rescue his people (Is 63:1-6)

    Israel's unrighteousness and helpless condition (Is 63:7–66:17)

Foreign peoples will come to God (Is 66:18-23)

The message of Isaiah in this closing section of the book is that God will rescue and restore his people, overcoming the problem that has plagued them throughout their history—sinful hearts, leading to idolatry and unrighteousness; a broken relationship with God; and a failure to live out their vocation in the world. The prophet now sees a people who shine with God's glory, displaying his righteous character and reflecting his beauty in the world. As the structure shows, Isaiah 60–62, which is all about God's plan to restore glory to and through his people, is the heart of this section of Isaiah and forms the climax of the book:

Arise, shine, for your light has come,
    and *the glory of the* LORD *has risen upon you.*
For behold, darkness shall cover the earth,
    and thick darkness the peoples;

---

[8]See John N. Oswalt, *The Book of Isaiah Chapters 40–66*, New International Commentary on the Old Testament (Grand Rapids, MI: Eerdmans, 1998), 452-55; Oswalt, "Isaiah 60–62: The Glory of the Lord," *Calvin Theological Journal* 40 (2005): 95-103.

but the LORD will arise upon you,
> and *his glory will be seen upon you.*
And nations shall come to your light,
> and kings to the brightness of your rising. (Is 60:1-3)

The revelation of God's glory to his people will render them glorious (Is 60:2). Like Moses, who was radiant after being in the presence of God's glory, Isaiah envisions a radiant people (Is 60:5) who reflect God's glory and shine with his righteousness (Is 61:3, 10), attracting the nations to the beauty of it.

THE GLORY OF THE NATIONS

When the nations are drawn to God by his glory shining through his people (Is 60:3), they will bring their wealth and glory with them.[9] In Isaiah 60, they come bringing the abundance of the sea, a multitude of camels, flocks and rams, the wood of cypress, plane, and pine trees (Is 60:6-7, 13). The nations will offer their very best as gifts to the Lord (Is 60:7).

This is a picture of humanity restored. God created humans to rule as his image, cultivating and caring for creation, drawing out life and fruitfulness from the earth and causing everything in creation to bear the marks of the glory of God. After the fall, humans began to exercise dominion and use their creative capacities for self-exaltation and evil rather than for God's glory and praise. Isaiah has proclaimed judgment on Israel and the nations for this, telling them that all their God-less glory will be brought to nothing (Is 10:18; 14:18; 16:14; 17:3-4; 21:16).

In the end, Isaiah sees a redeemed people shining with God's glory, and the nations bringing their best gifts as acts of worship: "They shall bring gold and frankincense, and shall bring good news, the praises of the LORD" (Is 60:6). With these gifts, God says, "I will beautify my beautiful house" (Is 60:7) and "beautify the place of my sanctuary, and I will make the place of my feet glorious" (Is 60:13). Jerusalem, which for Isaiah stands for the world under the rule and reign of God, will be filled "with peace . . . like a river, and the glory of the nations like an overflowing stream" (Is 66:12). As people are restored to their

---

[9]The glory of nations is a theme in earlier parts of Isaiah (Is 10:18; 14:18; 16:14; 17:3-4; 21:16), but in a negative sense, contrasted with its positive sense in the closing chapters of the book.

truly human vocation—offering up their work and their lives to God's glory and praise—glory will fill the earth as it was always meant to.

THE GLORY OF GOD'S SERVANT, SHARED WITH HIS PEOPLE, FILLING THE EARTH

Returning to our diagram, we can depict the overarching message of Isaiah like this:

Figure 5.1. The Messiah restores God's relationship with his people

A. Israel's story of distrust, disobedience, and dishonor to God is resolved in the Messiah. He is God's Servant, who will glorify God where Israel (and all humanity) failed (Is 49:3). He is the righteous one, who will bear the sin of his people and make many to be accounted righteous (Is 53:11). Through him, God's relationship with his people will be restored so they can know God in the intimate way he intended and be his faithful covenant people (Is 11:9; 54:5-10; 55:3).

Figure 5.2. The Messiah causes God's glory to shine through his people to all creation

B. The Messiah will bring God's good rule and reign back to his world—a rule of righteousness and justice that causes all people to see the glory of God (Is 9:7; 40:5). With him, God's people will also rule in the righteous way that God intended for humanity in creation: "Behold, a king will reign in righteousness, and princes will rule in justice" (Is 32:1). Through the liberating work of the Messiah, God's people will become "oaks of righteousness, the planting of the LORD, that he may be glorified" (Is 63:1). The ethical and vocational glory God intended for humans in creation will be restored. God's people will shine with his glory, and the nations will be drawn to God's glory through them (Is 60:1-3). And so "the earth will be filled with the knowledge of the LORD as the waters cover the sea" (Is 11:9). Through the Messiah and through his people, God will bring to pass the plan he instituted at creation and has reiterated throughout the unfolding story of the Bible: "The whole earth is full of his glory!" (Is 6:3).

CONCLUSION: HOPE FOR THE WHOLE WORLD

God announces in the closing words of Isaiah, "The time is coming to gather all nations and all tongues. And they shall come and see my glory" (Is 66:18). God will send his people to the farthest nations "that have not heard my fame or seen my glory. And they shall declare my glory among the nations" (Is 66:19). And so "all flesh shall come to worship before me, declares the Lord" (Is 66:23). Isaiah's vision is universal in scope. It centers on the glory of God, revealed through the Messiah, restored to his people, displayed among the nations, and filling all the earth.

These are the words that inspired Simeon many centuries later, who was waiting for this promised consolation of Israel. Isaiah's prophecies created an expectation that God would come to reign as king, bringing salvation prepared for all peoples. Through the Messiah, God promises to give light for revelation to Gentiles and to restore his glory to Israel so that God's people might once more share in and show forth the glory of God. Isaiah saw a day coming when the world would be full of the glory of the Lord, full of knowing God as the waters cover the sea. God's joy and life will fill everyone and everything. This is the good news the Fifth Gospel proclaims.

Chapter Six

EZEKIEL

THE RETURN OF GLORY
TO GOD'S TEMPLE

The latter glory of this house shall be greater than the former,
says the LORD of hosts. And in this place I will give peace,
declares the LORD of hosts.

HAGGAI 2:9

WHEN WE THINK OF PEOPLE who encountered the glory of God in up-close and spectacular ways in the Old Testament, a few individuals top the list. There is Moses, who entered the glory cloud that covered Mount Sinai (Ex 24:15-18). Later he asked to see God's glory, and God revealed his character to Moses in such brilliance that his face glowed with the brightness of God's glory (Ex 34).

There is Isaiah, who saw the Lord enthroned, "high and lifted up" (Is 6:1), surrounded by seraphim and smoke, as we saw in chapter five.

And then there is Ezekiel. In a series of visions, Ezekiel sees the glory of the Lord appearing (Ezek 1–3), the glory of the Lord departing from Jerusalem (Ezek 8–11), and, at the climax of the book, the glory of the Lord returning to dwell with his people (Ezek 40–48). The glory of the Lord is the most fundamental concept in the book of Ezekiel, so much so that these three visions give the book its shape and structure.[1] In this chapter we will trace the major movements of the glory of the Lord and see how the prophecies given to Ezekiel add another brushstroke to the prophetic portrait of a coming day when God's glory will fill creation.

EZEKIEL'S VISION OF THE GLORY OF THE LORD

Ezekiel, like Isaiah before him, has a vision of God that propels him into his calling to preach judgment to the people of Israel (Is 6; Ezek 1–2). Isaiah saw the throne of God, with the train of his robe filling the heavenly temple. Ezekiel also sees the throne of God, but his description is more elaborate (and more mysterious) than Isaiah's or any other depiction of God's glory in the Old Testament.

After the death of King Solomon, the nation of Israel had been divided into two kingdoms: the Northern Kingdom of Israel and the Southern Kingdom of Judah (1 Kings 12:16-20). By the time of Ezekiel, Isaiah's prophesied judgments had come to pass, and Israel (the Northern Kingdom) had been defeated by Assyria (around 722 BC) and ceased to exist as a nation. Now, nearly 140 years later, Judah (the Southern Kingdom) is facing judgment for their continued rebellion against the Lord, this time at the hands of Babylon and its king, Nebuchadnezzar.

In a series of sieges against Jerusalem, many Israelites are taken from the Promised Land into exile in Babylon. Ezekiel's first vision occurs while he is "among the exiles by the Chebar canal" (Ezek 1:1). In a scene reminiscent of the glory cloud that covered Mount Sinai (Ex 19:16-19; 20:18), Ezekiel sees a stormy wind, a great cloud with brightness around it, fire flashing continually, and what looks like gleaming metal in the midst of the fire (Ezek 1:4).

From the midst of the cloud, Ezekiel sees four winged creatures, humanlike in appearance yet each having four faces: the face of a human, a lion, an ox, and an eagle (Ezek 1:10). The creatures "darted to and fro, like the appearance of a flash of lightning" (Ezek 1:14). Beside each of them is a wheel, described

---

[1]Peter DeVries, "Ezekiel: Prophet of the Name and Glory of YHWH—the Character of His Book and Several of Its Main Themes," *Journal of Biblical and Pneumatological Research* 4 (Fall 2012): 105.

as "a wheel within a wheel" (Ezek 1:16), able to move in all directions, with eyes around the rims of the wheels. The wheels go wherever the creatures go, "for the spirit of the living creatures was in the wheels" (Ezek 1:20).

Later we learn that these creatures are cherubim (Ezek 10:15-16, 20). Cherubim are spiritual beings that are commonly associated with God's presence in the Old Testament. In Eden, the tabernacle, and the temple, cherubim guarded the sanctuary of the Lord (Gen 3:24; Ex 25:18-22; 1 Sam 4:4; 2 Sam 6:2; 1 Kings 6:23-29; 8:6-7; 2 Kings 19:15). Ezekiel sees above the heads of the cherubim "the likeness of a throne, in appearance like sapphire" (Ezek 1:26). Again we are reminded of Mount Sinai, when Moses and the seventy elders of Israel "went up, and they saw the God of Israel. There was under his feet as it were a pavement of sapphire stone, like the very heaven for clearness" (Ex 24:9-10).

In Exodus 24, there is no further description of the glory of God. Ezekiel says more. Yet as A. W. Tozer notes in his spiritual classic *The Knowledge of the Holy*, "The nearer [Ezekiel] approaches to the burning throne the less sure his words become."[2] Ezekiel's repeated use of the words *likeness*, *like*, and *appearance*, along with the phrase "as it were," communicates the mysteriousness of what he saw and makes evident that the glory of God cannot be fully seen or expressed. Ezekiel writes:

> And seated above the *likeness* of a throne was a *likeness* with a human *appearance*. And upward from what had the *appearance* of his waist I saw *as it were* gleaming metal, *like* the *appearance* of fire enclosed all around. And downward from what had the *appearance* of his waist I saw *as it were* the *appearance* of fire, and there was brightness around him. *Like* the *appearance* of the bow that is in the cloud on the day of rain, so was the *appearance* of the brightness all around. Such was the *appearance* of the *likeness* of the glory of the LORD. (Ezek 1:26-28)

Ezekiel's closing statement joins together both *appearance* and *likeness*, as if to say, "I really saw his glory, and yet I hardly have words to describe it." His vision makes plain that God has revealed his glory, and yet it is greater than we can comprehend. We are dependent on analogy to describe God, which

---

[2]A. W. Tozer, *The Knowledge of the Holy* (New York: Harper & Row, 1961), 15.

leads to approximations that, while true, are full of mystery and wonder. Moses had to be put in the cleft of a rock to see just a glimpse of God's back (Ex 33:22). Ezekiel is reduced to likenesses and appearances. The human mind cannot contain the infinite. The more we see of God's glory, the more there is to see, though we don't have the capacity to take it in. In the presence of such glory, there is one appropriate response. As with Moses in Exodus 34, and again with all the people of Israel who saw the glory of the Lord fill the temple (2 Chron 7:3), Ezekiel falls on his face before the Lord (Ezek 1:28).

In Ezekiel's vision, God is seated on his throne as the world's king, and he is on the move. It becomes evident in subsequent chapters that he is preparing to *move out*, leaving his people without his protective presence, giving them up to the full judgment they deserve. This revelation of his glory to Ezekiel becomes the prophet's ordination, as God calls Ezekiel to proclaim judgment to the people of Israel. Ezekiel obeys, and his pronouncements of coming judgment run from Ezekiel 2 through Ezekiel 24.

GLORY DEPARTS FROM THE TEMPLE

Five hundred years before the time of Ezekiel, King David desired to replace the tabernacle with a more permanent house for the Lord. God sent word to David through the prophet Nathan that David should not build a house for the Lord, but in fact God would build a "house" for David—that is, God promised to set a descendant of David on the throne and to establish his kingdom forever (2 Sam 7:1-17; 1 Chron 17:1-15). This promise is the basis for the messianic hopes and expectations so central to the remainder of the Old Testament. God also told David that his son Solomon would build the house for the Lord that David proposed, so that God might dwell in the midst of Israel and rule over his people. Solomon's temple replaced the tabernacle as the centerpiece of life in Israel. It was the place where God's glory dwelled (2 Chron 7:1-3) and where sacrifice and atonement for sins were made, enabling a holy God to dwell with his people.

Now, five hundred years later, Ezekiel prophesies that God is going to abandon this temple. He can no longer dwell in a "rebellious house" (Ezek 2:5)—a phrase occurring often in the book to describe God's people.

The temple, along with the entire city of Jerusalem, will be razed to the ground in judgment.

Ezekiel has a series of visions pertaining to the temple in Ezekiel 8. In them, he sees the people of Israel and its leaders committing idolatry, worshiping other gods and committing abominations within the temple complex itself. In the final of these visions, the Lord brings Ezekiel into the inner courts of the temple, to a place "between porch and altar" that was normally reserved for priests. Ezekiel sees a group of twenty-five men "with their backs to the temple of the LORD, and their faces toward the east, worshiping the sun toward the east" (Ezek 8:16).

The description of men who have turned their backs on the glory of God, choosing the glory of the sun instead, is shocking. Sadly, it is not so different from the human condition we witness throughout the story of the Bible, and in our own lives too. From Adam and Eve in the garden, to Israel and the golden calf, to Ezekiel's day and beyond, we have exchanged the glory of God for lesser things that can never satisfy or save.

Following the visions of Israel's idolatry against the Lord, Ezekiel again sees the glory of the Lord, as he had in Ezekiel 1. But now the glory is departing from the temple:

> Then the glory of the LORD went out from the threshold of the house, and stood over the cherubim. And the cherubim lifted up their wings and mounted up from the earth before my eyes as they went out, with the wheels beside them. And they stood at the entrance of the east gate of the house of the LORD, and the glory of the God of Israel was over them. (Ezek 10:18-19)

Finally "the glory of the Lord went up from the midst of the city" (Ezek 11:23). The departure of God's glory means the temple's and the city's destruction is certain, as God removes his protective presence from among his people. Still, while his people are in exile, God is graciously present among them as a sanctuary (Ezek 11:16) and promises one day to dwell among them again in their own land so they can experience the goodness of life under the dominion of their true king.[3] This promise of the restoration of God's presence and

---

[3]Thomas R. Schreiner, *The King in His Beauty: A Biblical Theology of the Old and New Testaments* (Grand Rapids, MI: Baker Academic, 2013), 373.

dominion is the subject of Ezekiel's closing vision, his third and final encounter with the glory of God.

YOU SHALL KNOW THAT I AM THE LORD

There is much that leads up to Ezekiel's climactic vision of the return of God's glory in Ezekiel 40–48. As we have seen, Ezekiel 2–24 contains pronouncements of judgment on Israel for her sin and idolatry. In Ezekiel 25–32, God's judgment is turned toward the foreign nations of the world for their wickedness. God will bring judgment on both Israel and the nations, but his judgment serves a larger purpose: "They shall know that I am the LORD" (Ezek 6:10). This phrase, with minor variations, occurs sixty-eight times in Ezekiel. Through God's acts of judgment, he makes himself known.

The same is true of his acts of mercy. As Ezekiel's message shifts to consolation and salvation in Ezekiel 33, the phrase continues with similar frequency. When God restores his people and makes their land once more "like the garden of Eden" (Ezek 36:35), both the house of Israel and "the nations that are left all around you shall know that I am LORD" (Ezek 36:36). This is God's grand purpose in making his glory known through judgment and mercy. All peoples will come to know that he is king. He is sovereign. His lordship will extend over all the earth.

We learn from Ezekiel (and from the whole Bible, really) that God is committed to giving his people—a people from all nations of the earth—what we most need and most desire. God is committed to giving us himself. More than anything else, we were made to know him. What else can compare? Who else can satisfy the deepest need and longing of our hearts? Only God himself, knowing him because he has made himself known to us.

> Let not the wise man boast in his wisdom, let not the mighty man boast in his might, let not the rich man boast in his riches, but let him who boasts boast in this, *that he understands and knows me*, that I am the LORD who practices steadfast love, justice, and righteousness in the earth. For in these things I delight, declares the LORD. (Jer 9:23-24)

This is eternal life, *that they know you*, the only true God, and Jesus Christ whom you have sent. (Jn 17:3)

I count everything as loss because of *the surpassing worth of knowing Christ Jesus my Lord*. (Phil 3:8)

Like these and many other verses in Scripture, Ezekiel's repeated refrain ("And you shall know that I am the LORD") highlights the greatest gift of God's redemption, the high calling and privilege of knowing the Lord.

YOU SHALL *SHOW* THAT I AM THE LORD

We learn a second, related truth from Ezekiel. As people come to truly know the Lord, he makes them what they were always meant to be—those whose lives display the truth of who God is and of his surpassing worth. Israel was supposed to glorify God by keeping Torah, reflecting God's character and nature, and causing the blessing of God's reign to come to all the earth. But they did the opposite. So God expelled them from the Promised Land and sent them into exile. Now, through Ezekiel, God promises to restore his people because of "concern for my holy name, which the house of Israel had profaned among the nations to which they came" (Ezek 36:21). In her unrighteousness, Israel had not represented God well before the nations of the earth.

Here we find a sobering reality. When a father is easily angered or harsh toward his children, when a husband or wife is uncaring or unfaithful to their spouse, when a boss or an employee prioritizes profit over people and treasures money more than God, or when someone fails to stand with and care for their weak and vulnerable neighbor . . . when we sin in these and countless other ways, we actually lie about and defame the character of God. God's people are meant to display the truth about who God is and what he is like. We are meant to reflect his glory, enabling others to see and know God. When we sin, we do the opposite. This, Ezekiel says, is Israel's great failure with regard to the nations. Because of their unrighteousness (Ezek 36:17-19) and because they had to go out of the land God had given to them (Ezek 36:20), God's name and reputation have been profaned rather than upheld (Ezek 36:21). But God will act to vindicate his name and his glory that his people have defamed.

God promises to redeem Israel by bringing them out of exile (Ezek 36:24); cleansing them of their sin and idolatry (Ezek 36:25); giving them new, soft hearts inclined toward trust and obedience in place of their hard, rebellious hearts (Ezek 36:26); and putting God's own Spirit within his people to enable them "to walk in my statutes and be careful to obey my rules" (Ezek 36:27). Then God will cause their land to become like the Garden of Eden (Ezek 36:35), and then the nations all around them will know that he is the Lord (Ezek 36:36). God's people will know the Lord so that they might show the Lord.

This great redemption—God enabling his people to know him and become what they were intended to be—is captured vividly in Ezekiel 37. God likens his people to a vast sea of dry bones strewn across a great valley. He tells Ezekiel to prophesy to the bones and call them to life. As he does, the bones begin to come together, and sinews, flesh, and skin grow on them. As with Adam in Eden, God breathes his breath into them, "and they lived and stood on their feet, an exceedingly great army" (Ezek 37:10; see Gen 2:7). God brings forth a new humanity from his people who were lifeless and dead in their sins. He promises to set his king over them and to reunite his people as one nation, with his presence in their midst:

> *My servant David shall be king over them*, and they shall all have one shepherd. They shall walk in my rules and be careful to obey my statutes. They shall dwell in the land that I gave to my servant Jacob, where your fathers lived. They and their children and their children's children shall dwell there forever, and *David my servant shall be their prince forever.* I will make a covenant of peace with them. It shall be an everlasting covenant with them. *And I will set them in their land and multiply them*, and will set my sanctuary in their midst forevermore. *My dwelling place shall be with them*, and I will be their God, and they shall be my people. *Then the nations will know that I am the LORD the who sanctifies Israel, when my sanctuary is in their midst forevermore.* (Ezek 37:24-28)

We see in this passage that the restoration of God's people centers on the work of the Messiah (the anointed king from the line of David) and the establishment of God's kingship over his people through him. We also see that God's presence will dwell with his people again, and he will multiply them, recalling the initial blessing and calling given to humanity in

Genesis 1:28. And we see the result of God's presence dwelling with his people and of their righteous character: everyone will know he is the Lord!

This section closes with a promise from the Lord: "I will set my glory among the nations" (Ezek 39:21) and "I will not hide my face anymore from [my people], when I pour out my Spirit upon the house of Israel" (Ezek 39:29). The nations will see God's glory. His people will see his face. This is precisely what the final, climactic vision in Ezekiel 40–48 is about.

THE RETURN OF THE GLORY OF THE LORD

In Ezekiel 40, God brings the prophet in a vision to the land of Israel and sets him on a high mountain with a city on it (Ezek 40:2-3). A man takes Ezekiel around the city, measuring the dimensions of the outer and inner temple courts and of the most holy place within the temple. The vision is reminiscent of the plans for the tabernacle God gave to Moses on Mount Sinai (Ex 25–31). But this vision, Hebrew Bible scholar Daniel Block explains, "is not presented as a blueprint for some future building to be constructed with human hands."[4] Rather, this temple "represents a new Eden, a cosmic mountain (40:2) where Yahweh dwells with his people."[5]

The scene before Ezekiel now (in Ezek 43) is the same as when God had departed from the temple in judgment (Ezek 10–11), only now Ezekiel sees the Lord returning: "And behold, the glory of the God of Israel was coming from the east. And the sound of his coming was like the sound of many waters, and the earth shone with his glory" (Ezek 43:2).

Wonderfully, the return of the glory of the Lord causes *the whole earth to shine with his glory* as it was always meant to. Ezekiel sees God's glory fill the temple (Ezek 43:5), and a voice speaks to him from the midst of the temple: "Son of man, this is the place of my throne and the place of the soles of my feet, where I will dwell in the midst of the people of Israel forever" (Ezek 43:7). God reveals to Ezekiel in this vision that a day is coming when his glory will return to dwell with his people, and they will live under his dominion once more.

---

[4]Daniel I. Block, *Ezekiel: Chapters 1–24*, New International Commentary on the Old Testament (Grand Rapids, MI: Eerdmans, 1997), 59.

[5]Schreiner, *King in His Beauty*, 384.

Perhaps the most striking and beautiful part of Ezekiel's vision is what comes as a result of the presence of God's glory within the temple. Ezekiel sees water flowing from below the threshold of the temple (Ezek 47:1). As the water flows out from the place where God's glory dwells, a trickle becomes a stream, and the stream becomes a great river (Ezek 47:5). Wherever the river goes, it brings life: "so everything will live where the river goes" (Ezek 47:9). Along the banks of the river are all kinds of fruit trees whose leaves never wither. They bear fresh fruit each month because they are watered with water from the sanctuary. "Their fruit," Ezekiel says, "will be for food, and their leaves for healing" (Ezek 47:12).

In Ezekiel's vision, God's glory dwelling among his people becomes the source of new creation life, spreading out and filling all the earth, bringing flourishing and life to all.[6] Ezekiel does not say much about how this will happen, though earlier in the book he hints at it by referencing the reign of the Messiah, the cleansing and transforming work of the Spirit, and the nations coming to know the Lord as a result of God's work among his people.

We see in Ezekiel what we have seen from creation onward: *God reveals his glory to his people, and he reveals his glory through his people, and so his glory will fill the earth, bringing life to all creation.* Ezekiel provides a fitting summary to his visions of a world dripping with the glory of God: "And the name of the city from that time on shall be, The LORD Is There" (Ezek 48:35).

CONCLUSION: GET READY FOR GOD TO COME

As history unfolds in the years following Ezekiel's prophecies, God does in fact bring his people out of exile, back to Jerusalem. The people begin to build a new temple, in hopes of the restoration of God's presence and glory, as Ezekiel had spoken. But things don't go as they hope. When the foundations of the new temple are laid, "many of the priests and Levites and heads of fathers' houses, old men who had seen the first house, wept with a loud voice" (Ezra 3:12). This temple, they can tell, is nothing compared with the former temple. The prophet Haggai comments: "Who is left among you who saw this

---

[6]The picture recalls the scene in Eden, the original dwelling place of God, and the river that flowed from Eden to water the earth (Gen 2:10).

house in its former glory? How do you see it now? Is it not as nothing in your eyes?" (Hag 2:3).

Haggai acknowledges the disappointment. He acknowledges that what they see with their physical eyes and what their hands accomplish cannot bring about the promised restoration of glory. And yet, the Lord tells his people that he is with them, working among them. He will accomplish all that he has promised:

> Fear not. For thus says the Lord of hosts: Yet once more, in a little while, I will shake the heavens and the earth and the sea and the dry land. And I will shake all nations, so that the treasures of all nations shall come in, and *I will fill this house with glory*, says the Lord of hosts. . . . *The latter glory of this house shall be greater than the former*, says the Lord of hosts. And in this place I will give peace, declares the Lord of hosts. (Hag 2:5-9)

God himself will fill his house with surpassing glory. As Isaiah prophesied, so now God declares through Haggai that the nations will come to the Lord, bringing their glory with them. A day is coming when God's house—now composed of the whole earth as the dwelling place of God—will be filled with glory.

We are never told that the glory of God fills the temple the people of Israel rebuild, as it had the tabernacle (Ex 40) and Solomon's temple (2 Chron 7). But the promises given through Ezekiel and others regarding the return of God's glory to dwell in the midst of his people still stand. In the final book of the Old Testament, God says through the prophet Malachi, "Behold, I send my messenger, and he will prepare the way before me. And *the Lord whom you seek will suddenly come to his temple*; and the messenger of the covenant in whom you delight, behold, he is coming, says the Lord of hosts" (Mal 3:1).

God is coming. Get ready for glory to return. This is the message the prophets announce. The way this will happen, though, is beyond what anyone could imagine. And so we turn to the New Testament—where glory himself comes down.

Chapter Seven

THE GOSPEL OF JOHN

GLORY COMES DOWN

And the Word became flesh and dwelt among us,
and we have seen his glory,
glory as of the only Son from the Father,
full of grace and truth.

JOHN 1:14

I LOVE GOOD STORIES. Some of my favorites are the ones I read with my kids. We usually read a chapter of a book together before bedtime, and often we will come to a high point in the story—a moment of tension or anticipation or disaster—when the author will abruptly end the chapter. That's the point at which I say, "Time for bed." And my kids respond in exasperation, "What?! We can't stop there. Dad, can you just read the first page of the next chapter? The first sentence? Just the first word? Pleeease?"

That's what reading the Old Testament is like. The story leaves us hanging. It is filled with tragedy and beauty, pain and promises, failures and hopes. But the resolution doesn't come. God's promises remain unfulfilled—promises of a coming Messiah who will restore God's reign and the goodness of his kingdom, of God dwelling with his people once more, of his glory displayed through them so that it fills the earth. These promises (and many more) are unresolved at the end of the Old Testament. When we come to its final pages, there's a distinct sense, "It can't end there!"

Then we turn the page to the Gospels. The Gospel writers, each in their own way, pick up the threads of the story and show how Jesus is the one the story was always moving toward and to whom it was pointing all along. His story is the continuation and climax of the story begun in the Old Testament. Through him the long-awaited resolution finally comes.

All four Gospels present Jesus as the embodiment of the glory of God and the one who brings the goodness of God's kingship to the world. However, it is John who most fully develops the glory theme in his Gospel, taking up many of the narrative threads from the Old Testament and showing how they unite in Jesus.

THE GLORY OF THE WORD-BECOME-FLESH

We only need to read the first verse of John's Gospel to recognize that John is writing a new Genesis, returning to the first creation account and opening a new window into it: "*In the beginning* was the Word, and the Word was with God, and the Word was God. . . . All things were made through him, and without him was not anything made that was made" (Jn 1:1, 3).

John gives a behind-the-scenes look at creation, telling us that all things were made through God's Word, who both was *with* God and *was* God. God's Word—the Father's only Son, Jesus Christ (Jn 1:14, 17)—was the one through whom God revealed his glory in creation. And now, John tells us, the same Word reveals God's glory through the incarnation: "And the Word became flesh and dwelt among us, and we have seen his glory, glory as of the only Son from the Father, full of grace and truth" (Jn 1:14). God's Word (his only Son) is the ultimate expression of God's character and heart. In the Word-become-flesh, we see God's glory in a way that surpasses all previous revelations. This is the great purpose of the incarnation, of God becoming human: he has come to *reveal* his glory to humanity and to *restore* his glory to humanity.

THE STORIES BENEATH THE GLORY OF THE WORD

Two stories inform John's theology of glory: the human story, drawn from the creation narratives in Genesis, and Israel's story, drawn from the Exodus narratives. But John also reveals a deeper story beneath both of these that gives rise to them: the story of the eternal relationship between Father and Son. Each of these stories gives shape to John's prologue (Jn 1:1-18), which in turn gives shape to his Gospel.

First, John presents the Word-become-flesh as the culmination of the human story. As I already noted, John begins his Gospel with the very words that open the creation account: "*In the beginning . . .*" (Jn 1:1; Gen 1:1). The climax of the first creation account was the making of human beings as God's image (Gen 1:26). The climax of John's new creation account is the Word becoming human (Jn 1:14). God created humans as his image to be his sons and daughters who would represent him as they ruled over creation. They were to fill the earth with his glory. But because of human rebellion, his intention for humanity was never realized. In the incarnation, God's eternal Son assumes our humanity in order to restore us to our intended glory. He is God's image who displays God's glory in his human flesh: "And the Word became flesh . . . and we have seen his glory" (Jn 1:14). In Jesus, the glory of God and the glory intended for humanity are beautifully united. Through him, the world in rebellion against God (Jn 1:10-11) is able to become what God intended. All who receive Jesus, John tells us, are given the right to become children of God once more (Jn 1:12-13).

Second, the Exodus narratives find their culmination in the glory of the Word. When John says that "the Word became flesh and *dwelt* among us," he is drawing us into Israel's story. The Greek verb translated "dwelt" in John 1:14 means he *tented* or *tabernacled* among us. God provided the tabernacle (and later the temple) for Israel as a remedy for the problem introduced in the fall. Adam and Eve could no longer dwell with God in the Garden of Eden due to their sin. The tabernacle made it possible for God's people to be in his presence (though in a limited way). In Exodus 40, when God's glory filled the tabernacle, God's dwelling place was once again with his people. But the problem of sin and idolatry continued until, as Ezekiel saw, the glory of the Lord departed from his sanctuary. Prophets such as Ezekiel, Haggai, and Malachi foretold a coming day when God would come to dwell with his people in surpassing glory. Now, in the Word-become-flesh, John announces that the promised glory has come. The Word has come to tabernacle among his people, "and we have seen his glory!"

The glory of the Word is "full of grace and truth" (Jn 1:14), a phrase that again recalls Israel's story. God revealed his glory to Moses on Mount Sinai, summed up in the expression "abounding in steadfast love and faithfulness" (Ex 34:6). The phrase "full of grace and truth" corresponds to that Old Testament phrase.[1] The very glory God revealed to Moses—a glory expressed in God's covenant love and faithfulness to his people—is revealed in its ultimate sense in Jesus, who has come from the Father as the consummate expression of God's gracious, unfailing love.

Additionally, John connects the glory seen in Jesus with the central place of the law (Torah) for Israel: "For the law was given through Moses; grace and truth came through Jesus Christ" (Jn 1:17). The laws given to Israel were reflective of God's character and his heart. They enabled Israel to know God and to display him to the nations as they lived according to his law. Now, John tells us, the fullness of the revelation of God's glory, seen in part through the law, has come through Jesus. The grace revealed in the law has given way to a surpassing and more complete revelation of grace through Jesus Christ: "For from his fullness we have all received, grace upon grace" (Jn 1:16).[2]

God's definitive revelation of his glory in the Old Testament was to Moses on Mount Sinai (Ex 34). His definitive revelation in the New Testament is in the coming of his Son, a revelation of the same glory Moses saw but in a more direct and intimate way. The glory seen in Jesus is "glory as of the only Son from the Father, full of grace and truth" (Jn 1:14). Just a few verses later, John says, "No one has ever seen God" (Jn 1:18), another allusion to Sinai, when God told Moses that no one could see his face and live (Ex 33:20). John highlights how different things are now that the Word has become flesh. "No

---

[1] Alexander Tsutserov, *Glory, Grace, and Truth: Ratification of the Sinaitic Covenant According to the Gospel of John* (Eugene, OR: Pickwick, 2009).

[2] The Greek preposition *anti*, translated "upon" ("grace *upon* grace," Jn 1:16), conveys the idea of replacement—the grace given through the law has been replaced with the surpassing grace that has come through Jesus Christ.

one has ever seen God"—until now!—"the only God, who is at the Father's side, he has made him known" (Jn 1:18). "No one has ever seen God," but "the Word became flesh, and we have seen his glory!"

John's rich trinitarian framework shines through here. This is the story behind the human story and Israel's story. All God does in creation and redemption flows from the eternal, intimate fellowship shared between Father and Son, a fellowship characterized by love expressed in the giving of glory (Jn 17:24). John conveys the intimacy of this relationship when he describes the Son as the one "who is at the Father's side," or, to stay closer to the Greek, "who is in the bosom of the Father" (Jn 1:18 ESV footnote). This one, who has eternally existed in the most intimate fellowship with the Father, is the one whose glory we see in the Word-made-flesh. He is the one who makes God known.

John, like Ezekiel, saw the glory of the Lord. But whereas Ezekiel's language is full of approximations and likenesses, John's is sure and certain: "The Word became flesh . . . and we have seen his glory, glory as of the only Son from the Father. . . . The only God, who is at the Father's side, he has made him known" (Jn 1:14, 18). Were we to ask today what Moses asked of God in Exodus 33—"Please show me your glory"—John would point to Jesus as the Father's answer to our request. "Look to Jesus! See in my Son the fullness of my glory." When we see Jesus, full of grace and truth, revealed in Scripture and made known to us by the Holy Spirit (Jn 16:14), we are in fact seeing the Father:

> And whoever sees me sees him who sent me. (Jn 12:45)

> From now on you do know him and have seen him. . . . Whoever has seen me has seen the Father. (Jn 14:7, 9)

The history of humankind, recounted in the Old Testament, is the history of human inability to see God's glory rightly and to respond appropriately—trusting and obeying him, delighting in and displaying his glory as his images in the world. The Word became flesh to bring resolution to that story. He has come so that "those who do not see may see" (Jn 9:39). He has come to heal our blindness so that we might behold his glory, believe, and have life.

SIGNS THAT SHOW HIS GLORY

Near the end of his Gospel, John gives the reason for writing the things he did: "Now Jesus did many other signs in the presence of the disciples, which are not written in this book; but these are written so that you may believe that Jesus is the Christ, the Son of God, and that by believing you may have life in his name" (Jn 20:30-31). Believing (or *trusting*, a term that better captures the sense of *believe* here), is the appropriate response to beholding God's glory.[3] The two are closely linked in John's Gospel. This is especially evident in the section of the Gospel that follows John's prologue, commonly known as the Book of Signs (Jn 1:19–12:50).

John recounts seven miracles (or "signs") of Jesus. In John 2, Jesus turns water to wine at a wedding in Cana, a miracle full of symbolic imagery about the coming fullness of the kingdom of God that Jesus is bringing (see, e.g., Is 25:6-8). John draws our attention to this as the first of Jesus' signs and declares the purpose of this and the other signs that follow: "This, the first of his signs, Jesus did at Cana in Galilee, *and manifested his glory*. And his disciples believed in him" (Jn 2:11).

Each of the signs John records is intended to reveal Jesus' identity and to make his glory known. The intended response, which we see here and in John 20:30-31, is that we might trust in him. When we behold God's glory, trust is the appropriate and natural response. This was where things went wrong in Eden. God revealed his glory in the garden, but the first humans (and all who followed after them) failed to trust him, which led to disobedience, which led to death. The natural response (trusting God) is no longer natural for us. In Jesus, this trust is being restored as the Son of God makes God's glory known and grants new birth (Jn 1:12; 3:3) that enables us to see his glory, to trust him, and so to live (Jn 20:31).

Immediately following Jesus' first sign at the wedding in Cana, John records an encounter at the temple in which Jesus drives out the moneychangers and upsets the Jewish authorities. They ask for a "sign" from Jesus to justify his actions (Jn 2:18). He responds not with an immediate sign but with a veiled

---

[3]To "believe" (Greek *pisteuō*) in John's Gospel is not simply to give mental assent to facts about someone (I believe Jesus lived, died, rose again) but to rely or depend on Jesus and to give him your allegiance. The English word *trust* seems to come closer to this idea.

statement pointing to what will be his final, climactic sign: "Destroy this temple, and in three days I will raise it up" (Jn 2:19). The Jews don't catch Jesus' meaning, but John makes sure his readers don't miss it: "But he was speaking about the temple of his body" (Jn 2:21). As he did in John 1:14, John here presents Jesus as the true temple, bringing to fulfillment all that the tabernacle and temple were pointing to. God's glory and presence now dwell in Jesus, and the sign that will most fully display his glory is his death and resurrection, when the temple is destroyed and he raises it up again three days later.

The culminating sign in this section of the Gospel is the raising of Lazarus from the dead. When Jesus receives word that his friend Lazarus is sick, he tells his disciples, "This illness does not lead to death. It is for the glory of God, *so that the Son of God may be glorified through it*" (Jn 11:4).

The purpose of this sign, as with all the signs, is that God's glory might be seen in his Son. And the revelation of his glory is so that Jesus' disciples might trust in him: "Lazarus has died, and for your sake I am glad that I was not there, so that you may believe" (Jn 11:14-15). Jesus allows his friends, whom he deeply loves, to grieve for a time (Jn 11:5-6), knowing he will raise Lazarus from the dead and his disciples will "see the glory of God" (Jn 11:40) and believe in him (Jn 11:42). John tells us that many do in fact believe because of seeing Lazarus raised to life (Jn 11:45).

Like the other signs, this sign points to a deeper truth about Jesus. Jesus tells Martha that her brother will rise again (Jn 11:23). When she acknowledges that he will rise "in the resurrection on the last day" (Jn 11:24), Jesus reorients her understanding of the resurrection around himself: "I am the resurrection and the life. Whoever believes in me, though he die, yet shall he live, and everyone who lives and believes in me shall never die. Do you believe this?" (Jn 11:25-26). Jesus has come to overthrow the reign of death and restore life. Lazarus's resurrection is a sign, revealing Jesus as the answer to death and the way to life for all who trust in him. And so the raising of Lazarus from the dead anticipates the climactic manifestation of Jesus' glory still to come in his own death and resurrection, where the defeat of death occurs and the true temple is raised up.

THE HOUR OF HIS GLORY

Near the end of the Book of Signs, following his triumphal entry into Jerusalem, Jesus says, "The hour has come for the Son of Man to be glorified" (Jn 12:23). Though Jesus' glory is made known in his signs, John has pointed toward a future, fuller glorification to come: "The Spirit had not yet been given, because Jesus was not yet glorified" (Jn 7:39). Jesus has lived with the hour of his glorification in view (Jn 2:4; 4:21, 23; 7:30; 8:20). Now it becomes clear that this hour, the time when Jesus will be glorified, is the hour of his death and resurrection, the two bound inseparably together: "Truly, truly, I say to you, unless a grain of wheat falls into the earth and dies, it remains alone; but if it dies, it bears much fruit" (Jn 12:24).

At the cross, Jesus' glory and the glory of his Father will be on full display. There we see glory full of grace and truth, mercy and justice. In his humiliation and shame, the Son of God shines with the glory of his Father's compassionate, merciful, saving, forgiving, self-giving love, with the glory of his justice, righteous indignation, and determination to overcome all that stands against his goodness and love in the world.

With this hour drawing near, we have something in John's narrative akin to the agony of Gethsemane and Jesus' prayer of surrender ("Not my will but yours be done"), which are recorded in the Synoptic Gospels. Jesus says, "Now is my soul troubled. And what shall I say? 'Father, save me from this hour'? But for this purpose I have come to this hour. *Father, glorify your name*" (Jn 12:27-28).

In facing his most difficult hour, Jesus' great desire is his Father's glory. This is the ultimate reason Jesus goes to the cross: so his Father's name and character, worth and greatness, will be known and honored. In response to his prayer, the Father answers from heaven, "I have glorified it, and I will glorify it again" (Jn 12:28). Jesus has the Father's glory in view, and so too does the Father. Through Jesus' incarnation and his signs, the Father has glorified his name. And through the death of his Son on the cross, he will glorify it again.

LIFTED UP TO DRAW ALL PEOPLE TO HIMSELF

In John 12, Jesus has God's glory in view as he approaches the hour of his death. He also has "all people" in view. When certain Greeks come desiring to see Jesus (Jn 12:20-22), it prompts his announcement that his hour has come (Jn 12:23). Sparked by the coming of these Gentiles, Jesus prays for the Father's name to be glorified (Jn 12:28) and then declares, "'Now is the judgment of this world; now will the ruler of this world be cast out. And I, when I am lifted up from the earth, will draw all people to myself.' He said this to show by what kind of death he was going to die" (Jn 12:31-33).

It's as if these Gentiles are the firstfruits of the "all peoples" that have been in God's heart through the story of the Bible. God's intention from creation onward, expressed first in the blessing and commission of Genesis 1:28 and then in numerous ways that grow out of Genesis 1:28, was that creation would be filled with the glory of God and that *all peoples* of the earth would experience the blessing of life under his loving dominion. Jesus is fulfilling God's plan, drawing all people to himself by being lifted up on the cross.

This "lifting up" (Jn 3:14; 8:28; 12:32, 34) carries the double idea of being *lifted up on the cross* and of being *glorified or exalted*. When Jesus is lifted up on the cross, his glory is on full display. This act enables the nations to see his glory and to come to him. Jesus' words recall Isaiah 52:13, "Behold, my servant will act wisely, and *he will be lifted up* and *exceedingly glorified*" (Is 52:13 LXX). According to Isaiah, the Servant is lifted up and glorified through his humiliation, suffering, and death for the sins of his people (Is 53:3-12). Jesus, through his death on the cross, fulfills the role of Isaiah's Suffering Servant, bearing our sins and bringing peace with God.

The story of the Bible has been about the revelation and restoration of glory to God's people, and through them to the whole world. These themes come together in Jesus, who reveals and displays the glory of God through his life and especially through his death. The hour of his death is the hour of his glory and the glory of his Father (Jn 12:23, 27-28). This hour opens the way for all people to come to him to receive life (Jn 12:32).

ISAIAH SAW HIS GLORY

The Book of Signs closes with one more reference to Jesus' glory. This time it comes in response to the unbelief of many Jews: "Though he had done so many signs before them, they still did not believe in him" (Jn 12:37). John explains that this unbelieving response fulfills two prophecies from Isaiah.

The first is from the Suffering Servant passage in Isaiah 53, "Lord, who has believed what he heard from us, and to whom has the arm of the Lord been revealed?" (Jn 12:38; quoting Is 53:1). The second comes from Isaiah 6, "He has blinded their eyes and hardened their heart, lest they see with their eyes, and understand with their heart, and turn, and I would heal them" (Jn 12:40; quoting Is 6:10).

John tells his readers, "Isaiah said these things because *he saw his glory* and spoke of him" (Jn 12:41). This is a stunning statement. John makes clear that the glory displayed in Jesus is the very glory Isaiah saw when he beheld the throne room of God and saw God ruling over the earth and filling it with his glory (Is 6:1-3). And it is the glory of the Servant of the Lord, who through his suffering and death for his people's sins is lifted up and glorified (Is 52:13–53:12).

That is why, when Gentiles come to Jesus in John 12, his focus turns to the hour of his glorification and "lifting up" (Jn 12:23, 32), which will come through his dying like a seed in order to bear much fruit (Jn 12:24).[4] This is the means by which all peoples will be drawn to him (Jn 12:32). In all of this we are seeing what Isaiah saw: the glory of God as exalted king over the world, accomplishing his plan to fill the earth with his glory (Is 6), which is one and the same as the glory of the Suffering Servant dying for his people and rising again (Is 53).

GLORY TO GOD, SALVATION TO ISRAEL AND THE NATIONS

Like the Book of Signs, in which the theme of glory formed bookends to the entire section (Jn 2:11; 12:23-43), glory also frames the second half of the Gospel, often referred to as the Book of Glory (Jn 13:1–20:31). In the opening scene, Jesus announces that the time for his glorification has come (Jn 13:31). The climactic chapters, John 19–20, narrate the death and resurrection of Jesus, which John has prepared his readers to see as the preeminent revelation of his glory.

---

[4]This was God's expressed intention for humanity, to be *fruitful* and multiply and fill the earth with his glory (Gen 1:28).

As we saw in John 12, Jesus has "all people" in view as he looks toward the cross. This focus continues in John 13, which opens on the night of his betrayal and arrest. After washing his disciples' feet and announcing that one of them will betray him, Jesus speaks of the moment that is drawing near: "When [Judas] had gone out, Jesus said, 'Now is the Son of Man glorified, and God is glorified in him. If God is glorified in him, God will also glorify him in himself, and glorify him at once'" (Jn 13:31-32).

Again, Jesus is thinking of his and his Father's glory as he moves toward his death. He is also thinking of the nations that will come to him as a result of his death. As he did in John 12, Jesus draws from the Servant songs of Isaiah. His statement "God is glorified in him" (Jn 13:31) borrows language from Isaiah 49:3, "You are my servant, Israel, *in whom I will be glorified.*" The Servant's role is to bring Israel back to the Lord (Is 49:5), but he will also be "a light for the nations, that [God's] salvation may reach to the ends of the earth" (Is 49:6). Here Jesus communicates to his disciples the same message as in John 12: his death is the means by which he will glorify God and rescue both Israel and the nations.

RECIPROCAL GLORY

The heart of John's theology of glory is the relationship between Father and Son.[5] Beginning in the prologue, John tells us that the eternal Word reveals "glory as of the only Son from the Father" (Jn 1:14). The Son eternally existed "in the bosom of the Father" and has come to make God known (Jn 1:18). The relationship between Father and Son remains central through the rest of the Gospel.

One of the striking features of this Father-Son relationship is the mutuality or reciprocal nature of their glory. Jesus seeks the Father's glory (Jn 7:18; 14:13). The Father seeks the glory of his Son (Jn 8:50, 54). In the Book of Glory, we learn that the relationship goes even deeper. Each receives glory *in* the glory of the other: "Now is the Son of Man glorified, and God is *glorified in him. If God is glorified in him,* God will *glorify him in himself*" (Jn 13:31-32).

---

[5]David Ford, "'To See My Glory': Jesus and the Dynamics of Glory in John's Gospel," in *Exploring the Glory of God: New Horizons for a Theology of Glory*, ed. Adesola Joan Akala (Lanham, MD: Fortress Academic, 2020), 15-26.

The glory of Father and Son are inseparable. In the Father's glory, the Son is glorified. And in the Son's glory, the Father is glorified. When we see the fullness of grace and truth (Jn 1:14, 16-17) in the Son, it is the Father's grace and truth we are seeing. When we behold the abundance, compassion, or authority of Jesus expressed in his signs, we are beholding the glory of the Father, displayed in his Son. When Jesus demonstrates sacrificial love and humility by washing his disciples' feet and especially in his death on the cross, he shows us the heart of his Father. The Father has given his glory to his Son. And the Son displays this glory so that all might know and glorify the Father. Their glory is *in* the glory of the other.

Jesus especially highlights the mutual (and eternal) nature of this glory in his Farewell Discourse (Jn 13:31–17:26). His last words to his disciples begin with a statement about mutual glorification in John 13:31-32. The discourse closes with his high priestly prayer (Jn 17), where his first words of prayer are about this mutual glorification: "Father, the hour has come; glorify your Son that the Son may glorify you" (Jn 17:1).

This is Jesus' heartbeat. He is the expression of the Father's glory, and in his incarnation, his signs, and all else he has done (culminating in the cross), the glory of his Father has been his aim. Now, as Jesus approaches his death on the cross, his own coming glory draws him like a magnet: "I glorified you on earth, having accomplished the work that you gave me to do. And now, Father, glorify me in your own presence with the glory that I had with you before the world existed" (Jn 17:4-5). We see here and at the end of Jesus' prayer that the glory shared between Father and Son is an eternal glory: "Father, I desire that they also, whom you have given me, may be with me where I am, to see *my glory that you have given me because you loved me before the foundation of the world*" (Jn 17:24).

The reciprocal giving and receiving of glory did not begin with the incarnation but has always characterized life within God. The deepest heart of God, existing before the foundation of the world, is love for his Son, and he expresses this love by giving his glory to his Son. The Father lovingly shares all he has and all he is with his Son:

> For as the Father has life in himself, so he has granted the Son also to have life in himself. (Jn 5:26)

All that the Father has is mine. (Jn 16:15)

I am praying . . . for those whom you have given me, for they are yours. All mine are yours, and yours are mine, and I am glorified in them. (Jn 17:9-10)

The love of Father for Son and Son for Father, expressed in their mutual glorifying of one another during Jesus' life on earth, is simply a continuation of the eternal relationship they enjoyed before creation. The Father and Son love one another, and this love is expressed in the Father sharing his glory with his Son and the Son radiating the glory of his Father.[6]

The Holy Spirit is also part of this fellowship. Jesus tells his disciples, "When the Spirit of truth comes, . . . he will glorify me, for he will take what is mine and declare it to you. All that the Father has is mine; therefore I said that he will take what is mine and declare it to you" (Jn 16:13-15). The Son glorifies the Father by making the Father's glory known. The Spirit glorifies the Son by making the Son's glory known. The Father gives what is his to the Son. The Spirit takes what is the Son's and makes it known to Jesus' followers. All of this is so both Father and Son might be glorified.

This story runs beneath the entire story of the Bible and is the bedrock beneath all that exists. It is from the fullness of life and love and fellowship and joy within God that he created the world, in order to make his glory known. And from this fullness the Father sent his Son, so he could re-create the world and fill it with his glory through his Son and through those to whom the Son gives his glory by the Spirit.

HIS GLORY GIVEN TO US

In his high priestly prayer, Jesus says to his Father, "The glory that you have given me I have given to them" (Jn 17:22). This means, on the one hand, that everything Jesus came to reveal of the Father's glory he has made known to his followers. Jesus reveals the Father's glory *to* believers.

But it means more than that. Jesus also grants his followers the gift of participating in his glory. He intends to reveal his glory *through* believers, and so he gives them his glory.

---

[6]The author of Hebrews expresses a similar idea: "He [the Son] is the radiance of the glory of God and the exact imprint of his nature" (Heb 1:3).

When we set Jesus' words in John 17:21 and John 17:22-23 beside each other, we begin to see the significance of what he is saying:

> that they may be one, just as you, Father, are in me, and I in you, *that they also may be in us*, <u>so that the world may believe that you have sent me</u>. (Jn 17:21)

> **the glory that you have given me I have given to them**, that they may be one even as we are one, I in them and you in me, *that they may become perfectly one*, <u>so that the world may know that you sent me and loved them even as you loved me</u>. (Jn 17:22-23)

In both statements, Jesus prays that believers "may be one." He describes this unity with reference to the relationship of the Trinity—"just as you, Father, are in me, and I in you"—and prays that believers might be "in us" (Jn 17:21). Jesus' prayer for oneness is, first, for believers to be one with God, brought into relationship with him and into the fellowship shared between Father and Son.

He continues to describe this unity in John 17:22-23: "that they may be one *even as we are one, I in them and you in me*, that they may become perfectly one" (Jn 17:23). The unity of believers results from being brought into relationship with Father and Son through union with Christ.

The thing that enables this union—and therefore this unity among believers—is Jesus giving his glory to them: "The glory that you have given me I have given to them, *that they may be one even as we are one, I in them and you in me*" (Jn 17:22-23). And his purpose is "that the world may know that you sent me and that you loved them even as you loved me" (Jn 17:23). Jesus gives his glory to those who believe in him as a witness to the world that the Father sent his Son and that the Father loves his people as he loves his Son.

The Father expressed his love for his Son by giving his glory to him (Jn 17:24). Jesus says that the Father loves believers with the same love. Jesus has given his glory (which the Father gave to him) to his people as a sign of this love, just as the Father, out of his love for his Son, gave his glory to him. Those who trust in Jesus become sharers in his glory who manifest that glory to the world.

BEARING THE FRUIT OF SELF-GIVING LOVE

What does it look like to manifest Jesus' glory in our lives? It looks like Christlike, self-giving love. Love is the fruit of our union with Christ (and therefore with the Father), the fruit of seeing his glory and sharing in it. Jesus emphasizes this throughout his Farewell Discourse.

In John 13, Jesus gives his disciples a "new commandment," to love one another: "*just as I have loved you*, you also are to love one another" (Jn 13:34; see Jn 15:12). Through his death on the cross, Jesus displays the fullness of his glory, revealing the depths of his and the Father's love. This both exemplifies and empowers the kind of love he intends to produce in his disciples. It opens a way for them and all people to return to God and be restored to what we were always intended to be: those who love God and love others from the heart. Jesus' followers reflect God's image and display his glory in how we treat others: "By this all people will know that you are my disciples, if you have love for one another" (Jn 13:35). This is what it means to be truly and fully human the way God intended.

In John 15, Jesus describes the relationship we are to have with him using the metaphor of a vine and its branches and says, "Abide in me, and I in you" (Jn 15:4). This is the mutual indwelling of the "I in them and you in me" relationship of oneness that Jesus prays for in John 17:23. If believers abide (or remain) in union with him, they will bear "much fruit" (Jn 15:5) and will glorify God: "By this my Father is glorified, that you bear much fruit and so prove to be my disciples" (Jn 15:8). What kind of fruit glorifies his Father and proves that we belong to Jesus? Jesus goes on to describe the fruit of sacrificial, self-giving love, the very love he will display on the cross: "This is my commandment, that you love one another as I have loved you. Greater love has no one than this, that someone lay down his life for his friends" (Jn 15:12-13).

This is what Jesus has in mind when he says, "The glory that you have given me I have given to them . . . so that the world may know that you sent me and loved them even as you loved me" (Jn 17:22-23). Jesus reveals God's glory *to* his people through his self-giving love on the cross. And he intends to reveal his glory *through* his people, as the world sees his self-giving love expressed in the lives of his followers. During his earthly life, Jesus was the tabernacle of

God, embodying divine glory (Jn 1:14).[7] Now his followers receive the glory God gave to him. They become God's temple, the dwelling place from which his glory is made manifest in the world through their love for one another.

Returning to our diagram, we can summarize the theme of glory in John's Gospel like this:

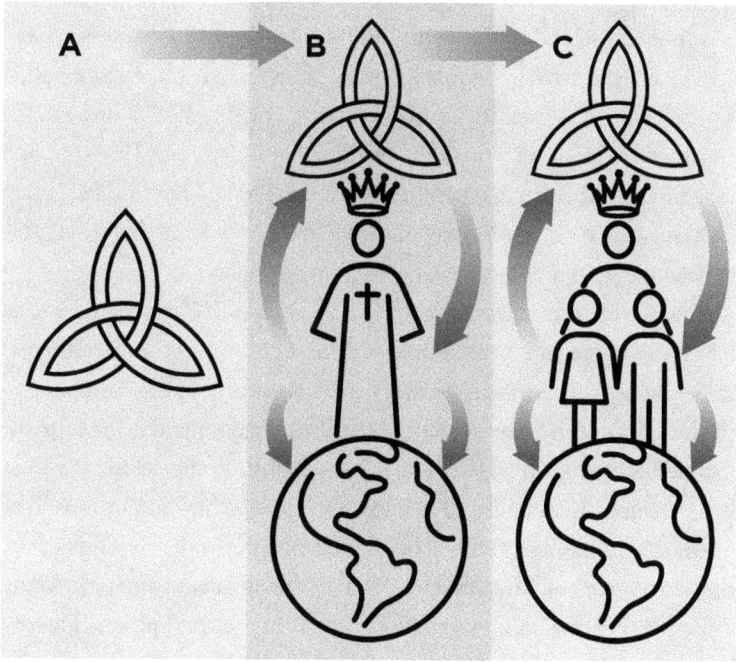

Figure 7.1. Triune glory revealed in the Son, and revealed to and through those who belong to the Son

A. The eternal fellowship of the Trinity is characterized by love expressed through a mutual giving and receiving of glory.

B. In the incarnation, the Father's glory is revealed to humanity through his Son. He displays God's glory in his life and in his death. By his sacrificial death on the cross, he demonstrates the self-giving love of God, overthrows the dominion of death, and draws all people (Jew and Gentile) to himself and to the glory for which they were created.

---

[7]Raymond E. Brown, *The Gospel According to John* (London: Geoffrey Chapman, 1975), 2:781.

C. Those who come to Jesus and put their trust in him become sharers in the glory of Father and Son. They are brought into fellowship with the triune God, sons and daughters who know him and see his glory in his Son. And they are sent by Jesus to spread the glory of his self-giving love to the world.

THE SPIRIT OF GLORY

It is in the mission Jesus gives to his followers that we especially see the activity of the Holy Spirit in John's Gospel. The Spirit is a gift from the Father and Son who will dwell within believers forever (Jn 14:16-17). Through the Spirit we are made alive with the resurrection life of Jesus (Jn 14:19) and brought into the "I am in my Father, and you in me, and I in you" fellowship with God (Jn 14:20). It is through the work of the Holy Spirit that we are able to behold the glory of Jesus and become sharers in his glory.

This is what Jesus has in mind when he cries out, "If anyone thirsts, let him come to me and drink. Whoever believes in me, as the Scripture has said, 'Out of his heart will flow rivers of living water'" (Jn 7:37-38).

Jesus draws this imagery from Ezekiel's vision of water flowing from the temple, becoming a great river that brings life to all creation (Ezek 47). Jesus is that temple. He promises that those who come to him and drink will be filled with his life, and they will become channels of his life as it flows from them to the world. John comments, "Now he said this about the Spirit, whom those who believed in him were to receive, for as yet the Spirit had not yet been given, because Jesus was not yet glorified" (Jn 7:39). The glorification John speaks of is Jesus' death and resurrection. When Jesus appears to his disciples in the upper room following his resurrection (Jn 20:19-29), he has been glorified, and the time for the gift of the Spirit has finally come.

In a beautiful scene that recalls the creation of Adam, when God breathed the breath of life into the first human (Gen 2:7), Jesus now says to his disciples, "'Peace be with you. As the Father has sent me, even so I am sending you.' And when he had said this, he breathed on them and said to them, 'Receive the Holy Spirit'" (Jn 20:21-22).

The Father sent Jesus to make his glory known, and now those who have seen his glory are sent by Jesus to do the same. To enable them to fulfill this mission, he breathes into them the breath of new life, the Holy Spirit. Those who are made alive by the Spirit are sent as God's new humanity, who have "rivers of living water" flowing through them as they carry his presence and glory to the world.

CONCLUSION: FOLLOW ME

The Gospel of John gives the ending to the story that the Old Testament left us waiting and longing for. That ending is Jesus. As the Christmas hymn declares, "The hopes and fears of all the years are met in thee tonight." In his incarnation, the eternal Word of God came into our fallen world and took on our human flesh. In him we see the glory of God we were created to behold, and through him we are being restored to the glory we were created to reflect. All who receive him and trust in his name become children of God (Jn 1:12), sharers in the very sonship of the Son ("I am ascending to *my Father and your Father*," Jn 20:17). He gives us his glory (Jn 17:22) for the sake of the world (Jn 17:23). He sends his followers into the world to display the glory of his self-giving love to all creation, so that the world might see his glory reflected in us and know by our love for one another that we belong to him (Jn 13:34-35). New Testament scholars N. T. Wright and Michael Bird capture the heart of John's message, saying,

> Because of the cross, Jesus offers us, here and now, his own sonship; his own spirit; his own mission to the world. The love which he incarnated, by which we are saved, is to become the love which fills us beyond capacity and flows out to heal the world; so that *the Word may become flesh* once more, and dwell (not just among us, but) *within us*. Having beheld his glory, *we must then reveal his glory, glory as of the beloved children of the father, full of grace and truth*.[8]

There is one final reference to glory in the Gospel of John. It comes in the epilogue (John 21). Jesus, in his merciful love, restores Peter to relationship with himself and commissions Peter to care for those Jesus loves ("feed my sheep," Jn 21:17). He then enigmatically tells Peter of the suffering and death that await him. When he is old, he will stretch out his hands and be dressed

---

[8]N. T. Wright and Michael Bird, *The New Testament in Its World: An Introduction to the History, Literature, and Theology of the First Christians* (Grand Rapids, MI: Zondervan Academic, 2019), 679, emphasis original.

by another and carried where he doesn't want to go (John 21:18). John explains to his readers, "This he said to show by what kind of death [Peter] was to glorify God" (Jn 21:19). Jesus then says to Peter, "Follow me" (Jn 21:19, 22).

This is a fitting conclusion to the Gospel that has shown how the Son of God, the Word-become-flesh, displays the glory of God in his life and especially in his death. So too for Jesus' followers. We have been chosen and appointed to bear much fruit (Jn 15:16), and we do this the same way Jesus did, by falling to the earth and dying (Jn 12:24), offering up our lives for the sake of the world. We are called to follow Jesus daily as he leads us in the way of sacrificial, self-giving love: "If anyone serves me, he must follow me; and where I am, there will my servant be also" (Jn 12:26). We his followers, recipients of his love and glory, get to share his love and glory with the world so others can come to know and participate in the life of the only true God and Jesus Christ whom he has sent (Jn 17:3).

Chapter Eight

ROMANS

THE HOPE OF GLORY

We have sufferings now. But the sufferings
we have now are nothing compared to
the great glory that will be given to us.

ROMANS 8:18 ICB

EVERYTHING CHANGED FOR SAUL OF TARSUS that day on the road to Damascus. One moment, breathing out threats and murder in his heart. The next moment, lying face-down on the ground, blinded and utterly disoriented by what he had seen and heard: a light from heaven and the voice of Jesus. Saul encountered what he would later describe as "the light of the knowledge of the glory of God in the face of Jesus Christ" (2 Cor 4:6). That encounter turned Saul's entire world upside down.[1]

Saul, whom we also know as the apostle Paul, was a well-trained Jew. He knew the Scriptures backward and forward. But like one trying to put a puzzle

---

[1]You can read about Paul's encounter with Jesus on the road to Damascus in Acts 9:1-19; 22:3-21; 26:12-18.

together without the picture on the box, Paul had put the pieces of the biblical story together in a way that caused him to view Jesus of Nazareth and his followers as a threat to everything he held sacred, a threat to the glory of God, for which Paul was zealous. That day on the road, the pieces were jarringly, wonderfully mixed up and rearranged, disoriented and reoriented. Blinded by the light of God's glory revealed in the face of Jesus, Paul began to really see for the first time. Going forward, Paul would tell the story he had learned from childhood, but in a radically different way. Now the glory of God, made known in Jesus the Messiah, would stand at the center of it all.

From that day on, Paul's mission was to proclaim the message of the gospel he had come to know through his encounter with Jesus on the road to Damascus, a message he referred to as "the gospel of the glory of Christ, who is the image of God" (2 Cor 4:4). Paul presents this "gospel of glory" perhaps most distinctively in his letter to the church at Rome. Glory is a unifying theme that runs through the heart of Romans, especially the first eight chapters of the letter. The essence of Paul's message is that *through the redeeming, justifying, reconciling work of Jesus, we have hope of sharing in the glory of God. This is what God always intended, and the restoration of our glory will bring restoration to all creation.*

THE GLORY-LESS LIFE OF ALL WHO ARE IN ADAM

When Paul proclaims the gospel in his letter to the Romans, he draws deeply from the story that has unfolded through Scripture to show that God's intention for his creation, and especially for humanity, is realized in Jesus and in all who trust in Jesus. Paul sees a unified plan that runs through history, a plan that is all about glory.

That plan began with creation. "For his invisible attributes, namely, his eternal power and divine nature, have been clearly perceived, ever since the creation of the world, in the things that have been made" (Rom 1:20). God put his eternal glory on display through his created world, but Paul indicts humanity for their response to the revelation of his glory: "For although they knew God, *they did not glorify him as God* or give thanks to him, but they became futile in their thinking, and their foolish hearts were darkened" (Rom 1:21 ESV altered). Who has done this unthinkable thing, refusing to give glory to God and respond to his goodness with gratitude? Paul argues in Romans 1–3 that all of us have. Jew and Gentile, from Adam to Israel to us—all humanity is in view.

Every human has "*exchanged the glory of the immortal God* for images resembling mortal man and birds and animals and creeping things" (Rom 1:23). Given the glory of God, which is of inestimable worth, we have turned away to worship all manner of created things in place of the Creator. In our ingratitude (think Adam and Eve, given "every tree of the garden" yet grasping after the one tree God withheld), we have turned created objects meant to direct our hearts toward God into substitutes for his glory instead. "Claiming to be wise, they became fools," Paul says (Rom 1:22).[2] None of us are exempt. This was Adam's story. It was Israel's story. It is our story.

The glory-less life of humanity is Paul's focus in the opening chapters of Romans. He blends together aspects of Adam's and Israel's story to show that no one is righteous (Rom 3:10). Jew and Gentile alike are under sin's dominion. All are "in Adam" and have followed in Adam's footsteps. This is precisely Paul's point in Romans 5:12-21, where the ideas he introduced in this opening section come into full bloom.[3] All are in Adam and, like Adam, have sin and death written over our story. But through the gift of God's grace, we can be joined to a different Adam, Jesus Christ, and become part of his story—a story with a new ending of glory and life.

That is where Paul's argument is going, but for now he hammers home his point that we have not embraced the revelation of God's glory and responded with the love, trust, and gratitude fitting for who he is. As a result, we have not glorified him by displaying his character and heart through our lives. Humans, created to know God and reflect him in the world, have "exchanged the truth about God for a lie and worshiped and served the creature

---

[2]Paul's words here recall Gen 3:6. Eve saw "that the tree was to be desired to make one wise."
[3]N. T. Wright, *Romans*, New Interpreters Bible Commentary 9 (Nashville: Abingdon, 2015), describes Paul's method in Romans using the helpful analogy of a rosebud that slowly opens until the full flower is visible. The entirety of the rose is present before it blossoms, but it is only as it starts to open that the contents of the bud can be more fully seen. Paul provides glimpses of the wound-up bud (in our case, portions of Rom 1–3) and then unfolds the flower so it can be more fully seen (Rom 5:12-21).

rather than the Creator, who is blessed forever!" (Rom 1:25).[4] We have glorified creation but not creation's Maker.

The result, Paul says three times, is that "God gave them up": "to the dishonoring of their bodies among themselves" (Rom 1:24), "to dishonorable passions" (Rom 1:26), and "to a debased mind to do what ought not to be done" (Rom 1:28). "Dishonor" (*atimia*), part of the word group in focus here, is a common antonym for "glory" (*doxa*).[5] It's as if Paul can hardly think of the affront to God's glory without also thinking of the inevitable loss this brings to our own. Made as the image of God to display the truth of his goodness through our lives, we have instead suppressed the truth about God through our unrighteousness (Rom 1:18).

FALLING SHORT OF GLORY

The actions Paul recounts in the opening chapters of Romans show that when we refuse to make much of God's glory, we suffer the loss of the glory he intended for us. That's the conclusion Paul draws in Romans 3:23, in a sweeping statement that brings his argument in the opening chapters to a crescendo: "For all have sinned and fall short of the glory of God."[6] We have all failed to give glory to God (Rom 1:21), and so consequently we also fail to exhibit his character and nature in our lives. That's what it means to fall short of his glory.

The way Paul reduces sin to its essence in Romans 3:23, defining it with reference to the glory of God, has proved clarifying and convicting for me time and again. When I have failed to treat others with honor or love, Paul's words in Romans 3:23 have been a beacon of light, illuminating my own darkness and showing it for what it is. At the same time his words light a path and redirect

---

[4]Paul borrows language from Ps 106:20, where the psalmist reflects on Israel's fall with the golden calf in Ex 32 and says that Israel "exchanged the glory of God for the image of an ox that eats grass."

[5]See 1 Cor 15:43; 2 Cor 6:8; also the Greek text (LXX) of Is 10:16; Hos 4:7; Hab 2:16; Prov 3:35; 11:16; Sirach 3:10; 5:13; 29:6.

[6]Paul uses the same phrase in Rom 5:12, "sin came into the world through one man, and death through sin, and so death spread to all men because *all sinned* [*pantes hēmarton*]." The effect of Adam's choice stands over the entire human race. All sinned because all are in Adam. And because all sinned, all fall short of the divine glory we were created to share in and reveal throughout creation.

my heart toward the thing for which I was made. I have not merely been impatient or unkind or proud or selfish. I have fallen short of God's glory. I have failed to be like him. I have expressed something less than the truth about who God is and what he is like and have acted against the astonishing thing for which he created me—participating in his goodness and self-giving love.

Seeing my sin in this light has a way of engaging my heart in repentance and reorienting me toward the most honored and beautiful of callings, that of being like God, sharing in and spreading his goodness in the world. That's the glory we were designed for, the glory we will one day fully participate in because of Christ's redeeming work in our lives. Romans 3:23 calls us back to this vision of our true humanity, redirecting our hearts toward our true glory.

A NEW ENDING TO THE STORY

That we have fallen short of God's glory is only the beginning of Paul's message. Romans 3:23 comes right in the middle of a passage that serves as a hinge in the letter, swinging open the door to the good news Paul proclaims: "For all have sinned and fall short of the glory of God, *and are justified by his grace as a gift through the redemption that is in Christ Jesus*" (Rom 3:23-24).

Paul's story is that glory lost can become glory restored (and glory surpassing even that of Adam's original glory). In Christ, our story can have a new ending. That message of hope is what Paul turns his attention to in Romans 5–8.

THE HOPE OF GLORY: ROMANS 5:1-5

The hope of glory restored to and through believers is the overarching theme of Romans 5–8. The two most important glory passages come at the beginning and end of this part of the letter: Romans 5:1-5 and Romans 8:17-30.

Paul opens this section with these words: "Therefore, since we have been justified by faith, we have peace with God through our Lord Jesus Christ. Through him we have also obtained access by faith into this grace in which we stand, *and we rejoice in hope of the glory of God*" (Rom 5:1-2).

Justification by faith—the amazing truth that God declares the unrighteous to in fact be righteous because of their trust in Jesus—became Paul's subject near the end of Romans 3 (and continuing through Rom 4). Now he lays out the results of our justification. Because we have been justified by faith, we have peace with God and access to his presence and his grace (Rom 5:1). This, along with the theme of reconciliation, to which Paul will turn in Romans 5:10-11, speaks of our restored relationship with God through Jesus. Because God has brought us into right relationship with himself through his Son, we have a sure and certain hope of full participation in "the glory of God" (Rom 5:2). Here (and again in Rom 8:30) Paul shows that present justification culminates in future glory.

The hope of *the glory of God* in Romans 5:2 stands as the contrast to and reversal of the situation in Romans 3:23, where Paul proclaimed that all fall short of *the glory of God*. Paul depicts redemption in Christ as the overturning of the fall and all its effects. The glory originally intended for Adam (created as God's image to reflect his glory) and for Israel (a corporate Adam called to display God's glory to the nations) has now become the hope of those who stand in the grace of God.

"We rejoice in hope of the glory of God" (Rom 5:2). Paul also says, "we rejoice in our sufferings" (Rom 5:3). The first makes sense. But why would we rejoice in sufferings? Paul's answer is that trials and afflictions are part of the means God uses to bring us to our full share in his glory: "Suffering produces perseverance, and perseverance produces character, and character produces hope" (Rom 5:3-4 ESV altered).

Suffering, perseverance, character, and hope are like stepping stones in a path that leads to our appointed destiny: glory! Difficulties in this life lead to *perseverance*, which Paul has already said is a mark of those who, through a new covenant work of the Spirit in their hearts, "seek for glory" (and so attain it) by *persevering* in doing good (Rom 2:7).

Perseverance, in turn, leads to *character*. More specifically, it leads to a tested and approved character (*dokimēn*, Rom 5:4), a term that links back to Romans 1:28, where Paul used the verbal form of the same word to say that humanity tested and found God unworthy (*edokimasan*) of being factored into their knowledge. As a result, God handed them over to a tested and disapproved (*adokimon*) mind, leading them "to do what ought not be done" (Rom 1:28). Through Christ, God is reversing all of this, producing in believers a tested and approved character (Rom 5:4) through perseverance in the trials and afflictions we face.

God's character expressed in believers now is a taste, a down payment of the full glory that will shine through us in the new creation. This is the *hope* that results from the Spirit's present transforming work in our lives: "character produces hope" (Rom 5:4). The reason this hope is certain is that "God's love has been poured out in our hearts through the Holy Spirit" (Rom 5:5). The Spirit's transforming work in our lives is evidence that we are loved by God and destined for glory.[7]

Afflictions do not universally lead to perseverance and tested character. They can also produce hardness against God and increase our selfishness and idolatrous tendencies. The difference for believers lies in the work of the Holy Spirit, who unites us to Christ in his death and resurrection so that we begin to "walk in newness of life" (Rom 6:4) and "bear fruit for God" (Rom 7:4). The present, transforming work of the Spirit is a precursor to our full share in God's life and character to come, and so it produces hope—specifically, the "hope of the glory of God" (Rom 5:2).

GLORIFIED WITH THE MESSIAH: ROMANS 8:17-30

We now turn our attention to the Mount Everest of glory texts for Paul, Romans 8:17-30. Were you to ask an audience of Christians what their favorite chapter in the Bible is, my guess is that Romans 8 would make a good showing. It's a chapter full of favorite verses and themes: no condemnation in Christ (Rom 8:1), adoption as children of God (Rom 8:15-16), glory that outweighs our suffering (Rom 8:18), the Holy Spirit's (and Christ's) intercession on our behalf (Rom 8:26-27, 34), the providential working of all things for our good (Rom 8:28), God being for us (Rom 8:31), more than conquerors in Christ (Rom 8:37), and God's love from which nothing can separate us (Rom 8:38-39). Any one of these is enough to make your heart soar. Put them together in one chapter, and it's no wonder Romans 8 stands out as one of the greats.

---

[7]For a more detailed account of the textual evidence in support of this conclusion, see Donnie Berry, "Groaning for Glory: Another Look at the Spirit's Intercession in Romans 8:26-27," *Journal of the Evangelical Theological Society* 63, no. 2 (2020): 289-91.

There comes a challenge with reading a chapter like Romans 8, though. Because it has so many wonderful, standalone verses that can be memorized and stored up in our hearts, it's easy to miss the way the verses fit together as part of the larger story Paul is telling. When you begin to see how the pieces work together, you get an even greater sense of how rich and wonderful Romans 8 truly is.

In Romans 8:17, Paul returns to the theme of the hope of glory, which he introduced in Romans 5. He finally comes to the point he's been building toward throughout these middle chapters of the letter. The passage begins with the promise that those who have become children of God are heirs with Christ "provided we suffer with him in order that we may also be *glorified with him*" (Rom 8:17). It ends with the assurance that those God predestined, called, and justified "he also *glorified*" (Rom 8:30). Everything in this section is about our future glorification and drives toward the big idea Paul expresses: *though believers suffer now, we will one day co-inherit the cosmos with the Messiah, sharing in his very glory, which will bring freedom to all creation.*

Between these two verses that enfold the passage with glory, Paul draws us into the Bible's story using three groanings to give the story shape. Creation *groans* (Rom 8:22), God's children *groan* (Rom 8:23), and the Spirit "intercedes . . . with *groanings* too deep for words" (Rom 8:26). As we follow Paul through the passage, it becomes clear that the groaning he has in view—creation's, the Spirit's, and ours—is a groaning for glory. Paul assures us in the passage's conclusion that this glory is guaranteed for believers. What God has begun in us, he will finish. All whom he chooses, calls, and justifies, he will see through to our full share in his glory. And so Paul speaks of it as if it were already done—"[these] he also glorified" (Rom 8:30).

But what is the glory Paul has in mind? And why is there so much groaning in anticipation of this glory? We find answers to these questions in the story Paul captures in the passage.

CREATION GROANS FOR GLORY

Present sufferings and current human "weakness" (Rom 8:26) are the reason for the groanings Paul describes. All is not as it should be or one day will be. It is true that, when weighed in the balance, the sufferings of this present time cannot begin to compare with the future glory that will be revealed in and through God's children (Rom 8:18-19).[8] It is also true that for those united to Christ by the Spirit (Rom 8:1-16), his story—suffering, then glory—becomes our own. Sharing in Christ's suffering is in fact the pathway to sharing in his glory (Rom 8:17), and the pathway is marked by groaning.

"The creation," Paul says, "*waits with eager longing* for the revealing of the sons of God" (Rom 8:19). And again, "The whole creation has been *groaning* together in the pains of childbirth until now" (Rom 8:22). Why is creation expectantly waiting and groaning? "For the creation was subjected to futility, not willingly, but because of him who subjected it, in hope that the creation itself will be set free from its bondage to corruption and obtain the freedom of the glory of the children of God" (Rom 8:20-21).

Paul is thinking here of the Genesis narrative—the dominion over creation that God intended for humans (Gen 1:26, 28) and then humanity's forfeiture of that dominion through the fall (Gen 3). We have seen how the psalmist referred to our creation in God's image as God crowning us with glory and honor, which he further defines as God "*subjecting* all things under [humanity's] feet" (Ps 8:7 LXX). In place of this God-intended subjection meant to bring flourishing, Paul says that creation was "*subjected* to futility." Paul is describing the effects of the fall through the lens of Genesis 1–3 and Psalm 8, showing how humanity's failure to rule as God's representatives and to reflect his glory throughout creation affected the entire created order.

The intended irony in Romans 8:20-21 is that creation, designed to be subject to the rule of humans who exercise the kind of sovereignty that characterizes God, has instead become subject to the very futility that characterizes humanity in their refusal to glorify God ("they became *futile* in their thinking," Rom 1:21). Adam and Eve's sin had cosmic consequences. The rift in their relationship with God that resulted from their distrust and disobedience led to a rift in every other aspect of creation (Gen 3:17-19). And so creation groans.

We hear these groanings from every thorn and thistle, every sickness and disease, every drought or flood, plague or pandemic, hurricane or tsunami,

---

[8]The comparison here is similar to the image Paul uses of "light momentary affliction" in comparison with "an eternal weight of glory beyond all comparison" in 2 Cor 4:17.

from poverty and decay and every other aspect of the world that reflects its captivity to futility and death rather than to fruitfulness and life. The disarray in the hearts of humans has led to disarray in the entire created order. Instead of thriving under humanity's Godlike dominion, creation "groans" under its "bondage to corruption" (Rom 8:21-22).

Because creation was subjected to futility through Adam's sin (Rom 8:20), it now longs for the restored dominion of its true kings and queens. We find the counterpart to the ideas Paul expresses here earlier in Romans, when Paul says that because of one man's sin, "death reigned" (Rom 5:14, 17), and again, "sin reigned in death" (Rom 5:21). Paul contrasts the reign of sin and death with a "much more" statement to show the new reality brought about by Jesus that will exceedingly overturn the fall: "Much more will those who receive the abundance of grace and the free gift of righteousness *reign in life* through the one man Jesus Christ" (Rom 5:17). This is the restored rule of humans for which creation waits and groans.

Creation was subjected to futility and to the reign of death, but it was subjected "in hope" (Rom 8:20). The hope, of course, is the very same hope Paul introduced in Romans 5:2, the "hope of the glory of God." For Paul, the end cannot be separated from the beginning. When the consequences of human sin were inflicted on all creation, God did not abandon his purpose to share his glory with humans and to fill the earth with his glory through them. A restoration of his glory to and through humanity was always where the story was headed. Now Paul paints a picture of the end of the story, an end that looks like creation sharing in the "freedom of the glory of the children of God" (Rom 8:21).

Throughout the passage, Paul casts the cosmic renewal in terms that recall God's universal revelation of his glory and people's rejection of that glory in Romans 1:18-25.[9] Paul envisions the renewal of the created order to be a reversal of Adam's (and all humanity's) sin, which is behind creation's current bondage to corruption. The destiny of the appointed rulers over creation

---

[9]Verbal correspondences between Rom 1:18-25 and Rom 8:17-30 include the creation/creature (Rom 1:20, 25; 8:19-22); glorified/glory (Rom 1:21, 23; 8:17-18, 21, 30); futile/futility (Rom 1:21; 8:20); image (Rom 1:23; 8:29); incorruptible/corruptible/corruption (Rom 1:23; 8:21); bodies (Rom 1:24; 8:23).

and the destiny of creation itself are indissoluble. Creation longs for "the revealing of the sons of God" (Rom 8:19), when God's glory will at last be put on display in and through us (Rom 8:18) and we will rule with Christ over the whole world, reflecting God's glory and bringing his goodness and life to all creation.

That's the inheritance Paul was thinking of when he introduced this discourse on glory in Romans 8:17 ("heirs of God and fellow heirs with Christ"). It's the inheritance Paul has already mentioned in Romans, when he spoke of God's "promise to Abraham and his offspring that he would be *heir of the world*" (Rom 4:13). Paul understood God's promise to Abraham to be about more than just the land of Canaan (see Gen 12:1-3; 13:14-17; 15:5; 17:6-8). For Paul, the Abrahamic promise is linked to God's original purpose for humanity to fill creation and to rule over it (Rom 1:26-28). This unified purpose of God runs through redemptive history—from Adam to Abraham to Israel—and finds its fulfillment in Christ and the children of God who are united to Christ by faith. We become co-heirs with Christ, bringing the freedom to all creation that will result from the restoration of glorified sons and daughters of God to their vocation in the world.

In an earlier chapter, I made reference to Disney's *The Lion King* as a compelling picture of God's plan for creation (the Pride Lands thriving and full of life under Mufasa's reign) and of what human sin did to creation (the Pride Lands filled with scarcity and death under the rule of the evil usurper Scar). Mufasa's son Simba, the rightful heir to the throne, was long supposed dead, and all hope had dried up in the Pride Lands. But then comes the best part of the movie, which echoes the part of the biblical story Paul is now telling. The wise Rafiki catches Simba's scent in the air: "He's alive!" The movie ends climactically with Simba's return to overthrow Scar and to bring prosperity back to the Pride Lands. *The Lion King* portrays the freedom and flourishing that comes from the rule of a good king. That's the image Paul paints in Romans 8, an image of Christ and those who are co-heirs with him, in the fullness of our true glory and ruling with Christ over creation once more. That's the glory for which creation groans.

WE GROAN FOR GLORY

"And not only the creation," Paul says, "but we ourselves, who have the firstfruits of the Spirit, groan inwardly" (Rom 8:23). We hunger and thirst for righteousness and ache for an end to the brokenness. We long for ourselves and others to be made whole, healed, and set free. That's the groaning. We groan for the same thing as creation, "the freedom of the glory of the children of God" (Rom 8:21), for us and all creation.

But Paul says it differently here: "We groan inwardly as we wait eagerly *for adoption as sons, the redemption of our bodies*" (Rom 8:23). The Spirit, who is the firstfruits of the glory to come—a guarantee that God will bring in the full harvest—is "the Spirit of adoption," who produces in us the very "Abba" cry of the Son (Rom 8:15; see Mk 14:36) and bears witness with our own spirit that we are children of God (Rom 8:16). The fullness of what it means to be God's children remains hidden while we live in our mortal bodies that are subject to death, corruption, and the subverting influence of the flesh (Rom 7:24; 8:10-13). There is a greater experience of our adoption to come, when the Father, who raised Christ from the dead *by his glory* (Rom 6:4), "will also give life to [our] mortal bodies through his Spirit who dwells in [us]" (Rom 8:11). That is when our full identity as God's children will be revealed to all creation. Creation waits with eager longing for this "revealing of the sons of God" (Rom 8:19). We wait for it too.

Jesus' appointment as Son of God in power through his resurrection (Rom 1:4) fulfilled the messianic promises of a human king who would exercise God's sovereign rule over creation. The resurrection of believers will also be our enthronement, when we are once again "crowned . . . with glory and honor" (Ps 8:5). Our present, corruptible bodies will be transformed (see 1 Cor 15:51-53), and we will share in "the glory of the immortal God" (Rom 1:23) in order to reign as image-bearing kings and queens in God's renewed world. God must fit us with bodies appropriate to the task—bodies of glory (Phil 3:21) like the very resurrection body of Jesus.

The resurrection of Christ—and the future resurrection of all who belong to Christ—is a reversal of the inverted dominion that resulted from Adam's sin, by which death came to reign (Rom 5:14, 17, 21). The last enemy to be destroyed, Paul says elsewhere, is death (1 Cor 15:26). "For as by a man came death, by a man has come also the resurrection of the dead" (1 Cor 15:21). Christ has already triumphed over death, and those who belong to him will share in his victory (1 Cor 15:23). This is precisely what Paul means when he says in Romans that we will "reign in life" (Rom 5:17). Through sharing in Christ's resurrection glory, we will no longer be subject to death. We will reign with Christ over creation in a state of resurrection life, exercising Godlike stewardship over his renewed creation and filling the world with life rather than death. Paul says that we were saved into this very hope (Rom 8:24). It is the same hope he has had in view since Romans 5:2, "hope of the glory of God." This is the hope of creation (Rom 8:20), and it is the hope of all who have been redeemed and justified by Jesus, united to him in his death and resurrection (Rom 6:3-5).

THE SPIRIT GROANS FOR GLORY

There is another groaning in the passage, the groaning of the Spirit. "Likewise the Spirit helps us in our weakness. For we do not know what to pray for as we ought, but the Spirit himself intercedes for us with groanings too deep for words" (Rom 8:26). "Likewise"—in the same way as creation and as believers—the Holy Spirit groans for our glory. And as we have already seen in Romans 5:2-5, the Spirit is active in bringing us to our appointed end. He is both the guarantee of our future glory (Rom 5:5; 8:23) and the agent of God's new creation life, imprinting God's character on the hearts of his people so we begin to walk in newness of life now as a preview of the glory to come (Rom 5:3-4; 6:4; 7:4-6; 8:1-16).

As we wait and hope for our coming glory, the Spirit "helps us in our *weakness*." By "weakness" Paul means the struggle he's been describing throughout Romans 7–8. We're people under grace, raised with Christ, and adopted as God's children. But we're also subject to corruption and wrestle with our old, "in Adam" flesh that is in alliance with sin and death. We're torn between two worlds—redeemed but still awaiting the fullness of our salvation.

That's why we groan. We feel the effects of the fall in our lives, and we long for the day when creation will be made right. We don't know how to get from present weakness and afflictions to our inheritance of glory. "We do not know what to pray for" (Rom 8:26), but the Spirit does. In our groanings, the Spirit is present, transposing them into intercession on our behalf. He intercedes for us "according to . . . God" (Rom 8:27), which means he intercedes in accordance with—and then acts to bring about—God's purposes and the forming of his character in our lives.[10] The groaning ache within us, often "too deep for words," is evidence of the Spirit's presence and work in and through us, drawing us and all creation into the freedom of the glory of God's children.

Right after these verses about the Spirit's intercession, Paul gives the wonderful promise of Romans 8:28: "And we know that for those who love God all things work together for good, for those who are called according to his purpose." The Spirit takes up the "all things" we experience—our sickness and suffering, our sin and failure, our wounds and disappointments, our frustrations and setbacks, all the pain and injustice we encounter in our lives and in the world around us. In his hands, they become tools to accomplish God's good and loving designs. God uses each trial to conform us to his Son's image (Rom 8:29). Through him, "all things" become servants of our eternal glory, life, and joy.

CONFORMED TO THE IMAGE OF GOD'S SON

Creation, believers, and the Spirit all groan, eagerly desiring our full share in the glory of God. And under the loving hand of God who has given the Spirit of sonship as the guarantee of this future glory, all things are working toward this end in our lives. This is the "good" of Romans 8:28, which Paul further describes as being "conformed to the image of [God's] Son" (Rom 8:29).

With this phrase, Paul returns to the Christ-centered nature of our future glorification that he began with in Romans 8:17, "fellow heirs with Christ . . . glorified with him." In Christ, we see what it means to be truly human. He is the image of God (2 Cor 4:4; Col 1:15), who perfectly reflects God's glory (2 Cor 3:18). He is the true Adam, who fulfills God's intentions for humanity. But he doesn't just fulfill them for himself. Paul's emphasis throughout Romans 8:17-30 has been on the participation of believers in the spoils of Christ's victory. Through conformity to the image of his Son, God is restoring believers to *our* true humanity

---

[10]Many English translations of Rom 8:27 say the Spirit intercedes "according to the will of God," but the Greek phrase simply says he intercedes "according to God" (*kata theon*).

and to the glory intended for us. The Spirit-produced longing in our hearts—to love more fully, to be free from sin's web and all its effects in our lives, to be more like God, more fully alive and whole, and to offer ourselves as a gift and blessing to the world—is in fact our destiny. Believers have been "pre-appointed" (*proorizō*) *to be conformed to the image of God's Son* (Rom 8:29), or, as Paul says in the very next verse, "pre-appointed"(*proorizō*) *to be glorified* (Rom 8:30).[11] To be conformed to the image of God's Son *is* the glory for which we were created and redeemed.

Our glory has both relational and vocational aspects. From Paul's recounting of the biblical story with reference to the glory of God, we see the following facets of God's glory shared with humanity.

A. First, there is a *relational* aspect to our glory. In Romans 8, our relationship with God as sons and daughters takes center stage in Paul's portrait of future glory. Because we are God's children, we are heirs with Christ and will be glorified (Rom 8:17). Creation waits for the revealing of the sons of God (Rom 8:19). Our adoption as sons and daughters, the redemption of our bodies (Rom 8:23), is another way of describing "the freedom of the glory of the children of God" (Rom 8:21). We are being conformed to the image of the Son, so that he might be the firstborn among many brothers and sisters who know his Father as their Father (Rom 8:29). While each of these descriptions highlights different aspects of our redemption and are more than relational, the relational dimension can never be extracted or discarded.

That the children of God become heirs of the cosmos is not just about receiving eternal riches or a position of authority in God's new world. It is Paul's way of communicating that as God's children, we share in all that belongs to the Father and to his Son. The "revealing of the sons of God" (Rom 8:19) communicates the idea that the privileged and intimate relationship of love the children of God share with the Father will finally be on full display before all of creation, and because of this relationship with him, we will finally be all we were created to be. Our glory is, first and foremost, relational glory. The children of God have been brought into a share in the

---

[11]Paul communicates a similar idea in Rom 9:23, when he says that "vessels of mercy" have been "prepared beforehand for glory."

Figure 8.1. The children of God will reign with Christ, bringing freedom to all creation

beautiful relationship of Father and Son through the Spirit, who even now is producing the Son's "Abba" cry in our hearts (Rom 8:16) as we wait expectantly for the even greater experience of this glory to come.

B. From this relationship flows a restoration of the *vocation* God intended for humanity when he created us as his image and crowned us with glory. The sons and daughters will bear the likeness of their Father, just as the Son always has. Our vocational glory includes *inward, ethical* aspects (Christlike character) and *outward, physical* aspects (resurrection bodies), both of which enable us to fulfill our royal role as God's images, created to display his glory in the world.

The Spirit is at work producing the character and likeness of God in believers (Rom 5:3-5) so that we will rule in a way that reflects God's loving and life-giving kingship. The Spirit is also the architect of our future bodily transformation. We will be united with Christ in a resurrection like Jesus' own resurrection (Rom 6:5), and God will give new life to our mortal bodies through his Spirit (Rom 8:11). The Spirit's "Abba" cry in us now is a sign that we are God's children and will one day receive the fullness of our adoption, the redemption of our bodies (Rom 8:23). God will fit us for life in his new world. We will share in his incorruptibility (Rom 2:7), no longer subject to death or to the influence of the flesh, so that we can rule and reign with Christ over his new creation.

CONCLUSION: GOD GRACIOUSLY GIVES ALL THINGS

As Paul brings the theme of the glory of God to its climax in Romans, he ends with the promise that the one who gave his Son for us will also "graciously give us all things" (Rom 8:32). What are the "all things" Paul has in view? Read within the context of Romans 8, it's the glory God has promised to those on whom he has set his love. No one and nothing can separate us from his love (Rom 8:35, 38-39), and so we will be glorified—fully and truly human, fully and truly alive, fully and truly united to God as sons and daughters who will reign with Christ over his redeemed creation forever. This is the great end to which God's love is leading us. This is our hope because of the rescuing and redeeming work of Christ. We will share in his glory, and all creation will celebrate and enter into the freedom of the glory of the children of God.

Chapter Nine

REVELATION

GLORY TO GOD AND TO THE LAMB FOREVER

To him who loves us and has freed us from our sins
by his blood and made us a kingdom, priests to his God and Father,
to him be glory and dominion forever and ever. Amen.

REVELATION 1:5-6

PAUL'S PORTRAIT OF FUTURE GLORY in Romans provides a glimpse of where human history is headed. The sons and daughters of God will share in the glory of the Son, and all creation will forever be under the loving and life-giving rule and reign of God. There are many other glimpses of glory in the New Testament as well.

GLIMPSES OF GLORY BETWEEN ROMANS AND REVELATION

To stay with the apostle Paul for a moment, he tells us over and over that the end of the story is tied up with glory—Jesus' glory and ours. The "blessed hope" for which believers wait is "the appearing of the glory of . . . Jesus

Christ" (Titus 2:13). Jesus will return "to be glorified in his saints, and to be marveled at among all who have believed" (2 Thess 1:10). In that day, Paul says, believers will "obtain the glory of our Lord Jesus Christ" (2 Thess 2:14). Paul prays that the name of Jesus may be glorified in believers and that they also may be glorified in him (2 Thess 1:12). When Christ appears, "[believers] also will appear with him in glory" (Col 3:4). Our salvation in Christ Jesus comes "with eternal glory" (2 Tim 2:10). This salvation is for Jews and also for Gentiles, those who have come to know the riches of the glory of the mystery God has made known to his saints, "which is Christ in you, the hope of glory" (Col 1:27). As believers behold the glory of Jesus, they are transformed into his image "from one degree of glory to another" (2 Cor 3:18). And the sufferings we experience now are "preparing for us an eternal weight of glory beyond all comparison" (2 Cor 4:17). For Paul, God's great story of redemption is leading to glory.

Likewise, Peter, in his first epistle, tells of present suffering giving way to glory. That was Christ's story, and it becomes the story of all who trust in him and "follow in his steps" (1 Pet 2:21). In the Old Testament, the Spirit spoke to the prophets of "the sufferings of Christ and the subsequent glories" (1 Pet 1:11). Now the very thing the prophets saw from afar has become a reality. God "raised [Christ] from the dead and gave him glory" (1 Pet 1:21). Peter writes this to remind persecuted Christians that this is also where their story is headed. They can rejoice when they share in Christ's sufferings, because they will also rejoice when his glory is at last fully revealed (1 Pet 4:13). The Spirit of glory rests on them in their sufferings (1 Pet 4:14). Peter himself is "a witness of the sufferings of Christ, as well as a partaker in the glory that is going to be revealed" (1 Pet 5:1). He reminds the elders of the church that they too "will receive the unfading crown of glory" (1 Pet 5:4). And he reminds all the saints that though they suffer a little while, "the God of all grace, who has called [them] to his eternal glory in Christ," will bring them to their appointed end (1 Pet 5:10).

The writer of Hebrews also reveals glory as the end toward which Jesus is leading those who belong to him. In Hebrews 2, the author draws us into the story of the Bible—to God originally placing creation under the dominion of humans. God's plan, the author of Hebrews tells us, is to restore that dominion. He quotes Psalm 8, referring to the way God "crowned [humanity] with glory and honor, putting everything in subjection under his feet" (Heb 2:7-8). We still live in a world suffering the effects of the fall, and we don't yet see everything made right and brought under human dominion (Heb 2:8). "But," the author tells us, "we see him who for a little while was made lower than the angels, namely Jesus, *crowned with glory and honor* because of the suffering of death" (Heb 2:9). By sharing in our humanity and suffering death for us, Jesus has received the crown of glory—the dominion— God intended for humans. And now God is "bringing many sons to glory" (Heb 2:10) through the work of his Son. "The world to come" (Heb 2:5) will be under Christ's good dominion, and we will share in his glory and his reign.

In their own ways, these New Testament authors point to a wonderful end to God's grand story that has to do with glory. This is also the case in the book of Revelation. The author of the last book of the Bible brings the biblical story to a close in a beautiful way that is wrapped in glory.

REVELATION'S SONGS OF GLORY

Revelation is a fitting culmination to the story of the Bible. The end of the story is directed toward giving glory to God, as it was always meant to be. In the opening chapter of Revelation, John writes, "To him who loves us and has freed us from our sins by his blood and made us a kingdom, priests to his God and Father, to him be glory and dominion forever and ever. Amen" (Rev 1:5-6). This is the first of many such expressions of praise. The unfolding drama in Revelation is filled with declarations of worship to God and to Jesus Christ. For example, the twenty-four elders who surround the throne of God declare,

> Worthy are you, our Lord and God,
>> to receive glory and honor and power,
> for you created all things,
>> and by your will they existed and were created. (Rev 4:11)

These same elders offer praise to Jesus ("the Lamb") for ransoming people for God from every tribe and language and people and nation (Rev 5:9-10). Then countless angels and living creatures join them in their song: "Worthy is the Lamb who was slain, to receive power and wealth and wisdom and might and honor and glory and blessing!" (Rev 5:12).

The choir continues to grow. John hears "every creature in heaven and on earth and under the earth and in the sea, and all that is in them" join the chorus: "To him who sits on the throne and to the Lamb be blessing and honor and glory and might forever and ever!" (Rev 5:13).

I said earlier that glory, as the Bible speaks of it, is God's very nature; glory is the revelation of his nature; and glory is the honor given him in response to the revelation of his nature. In these hymns of praise, we witness all creatures in heaven and on earth giving praise and honor and thanksgiving to God in response to the revelation of his nature in creation and redemption. The message of Revelation, and the message of the whole Bible, is that God is glorious—resplendently awesome and good. The fitting response to beholding his glory is to honor and praise him for who he is and what he has done. That's what we hear in the doxologies of Revelation, the song that will reverberate through new creation: *Glory to God and to the Lamb forever!*

GIVE GLORY TO GOD

Revelation shows us life as it was meant to be lived—a life of giving glory to God. It calls us into our true and full humanity. The phrase "give glory to God" is repeated throughout the book. In Revelation 4:9, it is the living creatures around the throne that give glory to God. All other occurrences involve humans. In Revelation 11:13, many are terrified at God's judgments poured out on the earth and "gave glory to the God of heaven." This is the ultimate purpose of God's judgments, to turn people from rebellion and idolatry so that they might glorify God, acknowledging his weightiness and worth, with the heart and life orientation that accompanies such an acknowledgment.

A few chapters later, an angel is sent to proclaim "an eternal gospel" (Rev 14:6) to every tribe and language and people and nation. His message is a warning ("judgment has come") and a summons to return to our created purpose: "Fear God and give him glory, because the hour of his judgment has come, and worship him who made heaven and earth, the sea and the springs of water" (Rev 14:7). Some refuse to heed the warning and persist in their rebellion. As a result, they suffer God's judgment. Of them it is said, "They did not repent and give him glory" (Rev 16:9). But those who turn to God and worship him become part of a great multitude of the redeemed, who, in Revelation 19, praise God because the consummation of history has finally come:

Hallelujah!
For the Lord our God
the Almighty reigns.
Let us rejoice and exult
and give him the glory,
for the marriage of the Lamb has come,
and his Bride has made herself ready. (Rev 19:6-7)

These words present a picture of life as God intended: his reign expressed in all creation, joy and the giving of glory as the response of his people, and the consummation of the fellowship with him for which we were created. This is where the story is heading.

There's a well-known Eastern Orthodox icon of Jesus' resurrection, referred to as *Christ's Descent into Hades* or *Anastasis* ("Resurrection"). It depicts Jesus standing over the pit of hell. Beneath him are chains and locks and the gates of hell that have held the dead captive, now broken beneath his feet. In the image, Jesus has taken Adam and Eve by the hand and is pulling them up out of the pit of death, raising them to life. That's a beautiful picture of what Christ has done for us through his death and resurrection. He raises Adam's offspring from death to life and restores our true humanity. Through him, we become what we were always meant to be: people alive with his life, who have returned to life in its fullness—life directed toward giving glory to God.

DOMINION OVER ALL CREATION: GOD, JESUS, US

The throne of God is one of the central images of Revelation. It is mentioned over forty times, and this reflects one of the main ideas of the book: God reigns in heaven, and he reigns over the earth. All that unfolds in history is under his control. He is accomplishing his sovereign purposes, and ultimately there is no rival or threat to his kingdom. Revelation is written to encourage Christians who are suffering persecution. They can endure their trials in full confidence that God will triumph over all enemies, and his good rule and reign will fill all things. This was his plan in creation. In Revelation we see his plan fulfilled in the new creation.

The throne of which Revelation speaks belongs to God. He is "King of the nations" (Rev 15:3), king over the whole world. But he shares his throne with his Son, who is "ruler of kings on earth" (Rev 1:5). Jesus, we are told, is "the ruler of God's creation" (Rev 3:14 NIV), the human ruler who fulfills the role God intended for Adam and humanity from the beginning (see Gen 1:26-28). Jesus is also the promised Davidic king, "the Lion of the tribe of Judah, the Root of David" (Rev 5:5). Loud voices in heaven proclaim words that are striking for their beauty and breadth, words made famous by Handel's "Hallelujah" chorus: "The kingdom of the world has become the kingdom of our Lord and of his Christ, and he shall reign forever and ever" (Rev 11:15). This beautifully captures the flow of history. God is drawing the kingdoms of the world under his rule and the rule of his Son. God's plan for his glory and dominion to fill the earth through his images (Gen 1:28) is being realized through the redemption accomplished by Jesus and his victory over evil, sin, and death.

In Revelation, God and the Lamb are not the only ones we see enthroned. We also see Jesus restoring those he redeems to their place as corulers with him in God's world. The Lamb who was slain has "ransomed people for God from every tribe and language and people and nation" (Rev 5:9). He makes them "a kingdom and priests to our God, and *they shall reign on the earth*" (Rev 5:10). Israel at Mount Sinai was commissioned to be "a kingdom of priests" representing God to the world and leading the world in worship to God (Ex 19:6). We saw earlier how this role was like the one he originally gave to humanity, whom he created to rule as his image and to fill the earth with his glory (Gen 1:28). Now Jesus restores his redeemed to the role God always planned for them. Jesus is King, and he restores Godlike dominion to his people: "The one who conquers, I will grant him *to sit with me on my throne*, as I also conquered and sat down with my Father on his throne" (Rev 3:21).

God's rule and reign will fill the whole world. Even now history is under his sovereign control and is moving toward the day when his glory will be fully revealed and made manifest. In Revelation, John is brought into the throne room of God, where he sees what Isaiah, many centuries before him, saw. Living creatures surround the throne, and day and night they never cease to say, "Holy, holy, holy, is the Lord God Almighty" (Rev 4:8). Those who know this song from Isaiah can fill in the rest of the words: "The whole earth is full of his glory" (Is 6:3). The time for the fulfillment of this great vision will soon be realized.[1]

GLORY FILLING EVERYTHING FOREVER

In Revelation 21–22, we are given a preview of that very thing. In this final scene of Revelation, the story of the Bible comes full circle. John sees a vision of what is to come, a vision of a new heaven and new earth (Rev 21:1). The dwelling place of God is with his people, as it was in Eden (Rev 21:3). All the effects of the fall are overturned. God has wiped every tear from the eyes of his people, and there is no more death or mourning or pain (Rev 21:4). The King, seated on his throne, says, "I am making all things new" (Rev 21:5).

Nearly every line of this chapter draws its images and language from the Old Testament. All the threads of the story are coming together now. We see a city, new Jerusalem, that comes down from heaven and becomes the centerpiece of God's new creation (Rev 21:2, 10). The city, which represents God's redeemed people, is referred to as "the Bride, the wife of the Lamb" (Rev 21:9; see Rev 19:7; 21:2). The intimacy and fellowship that God desires with his people is finally consummated in the new creation. When John sees the city (the Bride, the redeemed people of God), he sees it "coming down out of heaven from God, *having the glory of God*" (Rev 21:10-11). God's redeemed people are now characterized by his glory.

Previously in Revelation, when John beheld God, seated on his heavenly throne, he described his appearance as being "like jasper and carnelian, and around the throne was a rainbow that had the appearance of an emerald" (Rev 4:3). John draws imagery from what he knows as he attempts to describe the beauty, the colors, and the brightness of God's glory, which is beyond description. Jewels and precious stones provide the closest parallel to the radiance the biblical authors behold when they see God's glory.[2] In

---

[1] Stephen G. Dempster, *The Return of the Kingdom: A Biblical Theology of God's Reign*, Essential Studies in Biblical Theology (Downers Grove, IL: IVP Academic, 2024), 194.

[2] See, for example, Ex 24:10, "And they saw the God of Israel. There was under his feet as it were a pavement of sapphire stone, like the very heaven for clearness." John's descriptions are also

Revelation 21, John sees the same glory that he beheld in the heavenly vision of Revelation 4, only now God's glory has come from heaven to earth and is filling new creation through his people, whom John refers to as "the holy city Jerusalem . . . having the glory of God, its radiance like a most rare jewel, like a jasper, clear as crystal" (Rev 21:10-11). "The city," John says, "was pure gold, like clear glass" (Rev 21:18). Imagine a world dripping with God's glory, full of the color of his goodness, wisdom, and love, shining with his life and beauty, beaming with the brightness of his character and nature that fills everyone and everything. That's the picture John sees, and the closest thing to which he can compare it is precious stones (yet beyond our experience, which "gold, like clear glass" seems to signify), refracting the light of God's goodness in a stunning display of brilliance.

The fullness of God's character and presence is manifest in this new creation city, and the city seems to fill the whole world. It is described the way the temple in the Old Testament was described. But it's not a temple, John tells us, because the whole world has become God's dwelling place now. There is no longer any need for a temple. God's glory, which filled the temple in the Old Testament, now fills everything. In this city, "its temple is the Lord God the Almighty and the Lamb" (Rev 21:22). There is no need of sun or moon to shine in it, "for the glory of God gives it light, and its lamp is the Lamb" (Rev 21:23). The nations of the earth walk in the light of God's glory, "and the kings of the earth will bring their glory into it. . . . They will bring into it the glory and the honor of the nations" (Rev 21:24, 26). Here is a picture of humans fulfilling their royal destiny. Their creative, culture-making dominion is in service of the glory of God. They offer the work of their hands, which bears the imprint of God's glory, back to him in worship and praise.

BACK TO THE BEGINNING, ONLY BETTER AND BEYOND

Near the end of John's vision of the coming new creation, we find ourselves once more in a garden. With imagery drawn from Genesis 2 and from Ezekiel's great vision of the river that flowed from the threshold of the sanctuary (Ezek 47), John describes "the river of the water of life, bright as crystal,

---

reminiscent of Ezekiel's visions of the glory of the Lord, similarly described with imagery of precious stones, brightness, and colors shining all around (Ezek 1:26, 28; 10:1).

flowing from the throne of God and of the Lamb through the middle of the street of the city" (Rev 22:1-2). That this river flows from God's throne vividly captures a key idea we have emphasized throughout this study. The rule of God is a good, life-giving rule. Here in the new creation, we witness the life that flows out from God's kingship over the whole world. On either side of the river is the tree of life, with twelve kinds of fruit and leaves that are "for the healing of the nations" (Rev 22:2). The restoration of God's dominion over creation (which has come through the triumph of the Lamb) brings healing and life to everyone and everything who become part of God's new creation kingdom.

There is nothing "accursed" in this garden (Rev 22:3). The serpent of Genesis 3 (who is the great dragon of Revelation) has been defeated and has no access to God's new creation or his people (Rev 20:10). The curse of sin and death is no more. The throne of God and of the Lamb is in this garden-city (Rev 22:3). His loving and life-giving rule is over everything now, as it was always meant to be. His servants "will see his face, and his name will be on their foreheads" (Rev 22:4). This is language drawn from the high priest in Exodus, who had access to God's presence and who carried the Lord's name on his forehead, inscribed on the priestly turban (Ex 28:36-38).

But it reaches back further than that, all the way to Eden. God's people dwelled in his presence and were able to behold him in the garden. They were his images in the world, reflecting his character and displaying his glory. Here, in John's vision of the coming new creation, is a picture of this fellowship with God restored. God's people behold him ("they will see his face"), and they reflect him as they were meant to ("his name will be on their foreheads"). His people are crowned with the glory he intended for them, and sure enough, God's resurrected servants "will reign forever and ever" (Rev 22:5).

CONCLUSION: COME, LORD JESUS!

And so the end of the story is like the beginning, only better. "Even better than Eden," as one author says.[3] The whole story is about the triune God and his self-giving love spilling into his world, flowing to and through his people. God's design in creation was human beings who are truly good, with

---

[3]Nancy Guthrie, *Even Better Than Eden* (Wheaton, IL: Crossway, 2018).

hearts like the King's, who share in and reflect his glory. This is the pathway to joy. All our sorrows result from failures—on our part and on the part of others—to be *with* God and to be *like* God in the way he intended for us. But when we are with God, and when true goodness flows freely from our hearts, it is exhilarating. It feels like being truly alive, the way we were meant to be. This is the glory we were made for. This is the glory we will fully know in God's new creation.

God's people beholding his glory. God's people reflecting his glory. God's people ruling and reigning with him over new creation, filling the whole world with his glory. This is the end of the story, which is really the story's new beginning for which we are waiting and hoping.

> He who testifies to these things says,
> "Surely I am coming soon." Amen. Come, Lord Jesus.
>
> **REVELATION 22:20**

CONCLUSION

BEHOLDING AND BECOMING

THE BIBLE BEGINS with a human couple in a garden enjoying fellowship with God, alive with his life. It ends with human beings in a garden-like city, once more enjoying fellowship with God, fully alive with his life. Irenaeus of Lyons, a second-century church father, writes about this fellowship with God that is the source of our life: "For as His greatness is past finding out, so also His goodness is beyond expression; by which having been seen, He bestows life upon those who see Him. It is not possible to live apart from life, and the means of life is found in fellowship with God; but fellowship with God is to know God, and to enjoy His goodness."[1]

Irenaeus goes on to connect this life-giving fellowship with God's glory. He famously remarks, "For the glory of God is a living man; and the life of man consists in beholding God."[2] Irenaeus understood that the clearest expression of God's glory was a human being fully alive with the life of God. And how does one come to share in God's life and so reflect his glory? By

---

[1] Irenaeus of Lyons, *Against Heresies* 4.20.5. Translations from this work follow Alexander Roberts and William Rambaut, trans., *Ante-Nicene Fathers*, vol. 1, ed. Alexander Roberts, James Donaldson, and A. Cleveland Coxe (Buffalo, NY: Christian Literature, 1885), rev. and ed. for New Advent by Kevin Knight, www.newadvent.org/fathers/0103.htm.

[2] Irenaeus of Lyons, *Against Heresies* 4.20.7.

beholding him. When a person knows God and bows beneath the weight of his glory, experiencing his goodness and grace, that person comes alive. As a result, they become a living expression of God in the world. God created human beings for this kind of life. And in Christ he restores us to this life.[3]

TRANSFORMED BY BEHOLDING GLORY

God's glory is the source of our life and the source of our greatest joy. We were made to see, know, and delight in God's glory. It is in contemplating the glory of God that we are freed, little by little, from our preoccupation with lesser things. Our anxieties and fears start to lose their grip. Our hearts come alive. And all things begin to find their proper place in light of him.

The apostle Paul says, "We all, with unveiled face, beholding the glory of the Lord, are being transformed into the same image from one degree of glory to another" (2 Cor 3:18). That's a huge statement. How does transformation happen in our lives? By beholding the glory of the Lord. As we see him, we become like him.

This means that glory is not just a future hope. It is something we can begin to experience now, in the present, as we await the coming fullness of glory. How, though, do we behold God's glory today? This is a question worthy of more than a little thought. If, as Paul, Irenaeus, and so many others in the Bible and through history claim, God's glory is the source of our life, the power for transformation, and our greatest joy, then beholding his glory is of supreme importance.

It is the work of the Holy Spirit to reveal God's glory to us, and through that vision of his glory to transform us from glory to glory ("this comes from the Lord who is the Spirit," 2 Cor 3:18). The Spirit reveals God's glory to us in the pages of Scripture—in God's mighty acts of creation and deliverance; his words and works that express his righteous character, faithfulness, and justice; his redeeming love and grace presented in the unfolding story of the Bible; and especially in his Son, as we gaze on him in the Gospels and behold the glory of his humble incarnation, his perfect trust and obedience toward

---

[3]Irenaeus (*Against Heresies* 4.20.7) continues, "For if the manifestation of God which is made by means of the creation, affords life to all living in the earth, much more does that revelation of the Father which comes through the Word, give life to those who see God."

his Father, his love and grace toward sinners, his mercy and might as he heals and restores the lives of men and women, his authoritative teachings, his sacrificial laying down of his life, his triumphantly taking it up again, and his kingly ascension, intercession at the Father's right hand, and pouring out his Spirit upon believers, enabling us to see and to share the glory of God.[4] These revelations of glory in the Bible are the foundation for all true and trustworthy knowing of God.

We can also behold God's glory in nature, in the things he has made, which carry the imprint of his attributes. And we can behold his glory in people, created as his image to reflect his glory—in the spiritual gifts, creativity, and skills of individuals expressed in humble, beautiful, and awe-inspiring ways; in the work of men's and women's hands that contributes blessing and goodness to the world; in acts of kindness and generosity. We can behold his glory in art and music, and in stories people tell through books or movies that echo the true story and give expression to facets of God's character and heart. We can experience his glory in the friendship of others, their sacrificial love, their costly forgiveness. We can behold his glory in answered prayer and in God's providential orchestrating of events and circumstances that leave us in awe of his sovereignty, wisdom, and care for us. In these and many other ways, we are able to behold the glory of the Lord.

Our beholding on this side of the new heavens and new earth is sometimes dim and certainly partial (1 Cor 13:12). So too is our reflecting of his glory. But it is real. As the Spirit leads us into knowing and beholding "the glory of God in the face of Jesus Christ" (2 Cor 4:6), his life really does fill us and flow through us, however small and imperceptible it may at times seem.

When we see and experience the kindness and compassion of God for us, we become kinder and more compassionate toward others. When we are gripped by the revelation of God's sovereignty, strength, and loving care for us, it becomes easier to trust him, surrender our fears, and relinquish our destructive desires for control. On and on we could multiply examples.

This has implications for our relationships, our families, our work, our societies, and every facet of life. As we etch on these things the marks of love

---

[4]Not just the Gospels, however, but the whole Bible testifies of him. See Lk 24:27, 44-45; Jn 5:39-40, 46.

and generosity, justice and beauty, wisdom and goodness, which we have experienced from God, we are stepping into our high calling of being glory-spreading kings and queens over God's world. Our small, imperfect acts of Godlike, self-giving love become previews of the goodness God is leading us and all creation toward—filling the earth with the glory of the Lord as the waters cover the sea (Hab 2:14).

SEEING AND SHOWING, DELIGHTING AND DISPLAYING

The biblical story presents twin themes that have taken hold of me, which you have probably picked up on if you've read this far: *seeing* God's glory and *showing* his glory. Or, said differently, *delighting in* and *displaying* his glory. This is what we were made for, and it is meant to shape our understanding of who we are, why we exist, and why everything else exists too.

God created us to know him—to know his heart, his character, his greatness, and to be captivated by his glory. And he created us to be like him, displaying his glory in all we do and causing everything in creation to bear the imprint of his glory. We fall short of this in countless ways. But even then, our repentance can be informed and clarified by this understanding of God's glory, which calls us back to God and to our true purpose, inviting us into a story more wonderful than we can imagine.

I find myself often praying—for myself, for my family, and for others I know—along the lines of these twin themes: "God, open our eyes to see your glory; and as we do, may our lives shine with your glory."

That is my prayer for you.

> Now to him who is able to do far more abundantly than
> all that we ask or think, according to the power at work within us,
> to him be glory in the church and in Christ Jesus
> throughout all generations, forever and ever. Amen.
>
> **EPHESIANS 3:20-21**

ACKNOWLEDGMENTS

MANY HANDS MAKE LIGHT WORK, the saying goes. From my experience writing this book, I might alter the saying: many hands make better work. The work didn't always feel light, but because of the team of people who devoted their time, encouragement, sharp thinking, and editorial skills, the finished product is far better than it might otherwise have been.

I'm thankful to the following individuals for your investment in this project and, even more so, for your friendship: Clay Spencer, Luke Rawlings, Drew Clark, and Kaleb Watkins. The process of writing this book was a much richer experience because of your help and support along the way. I'm also thankful for my colleagues at Training Leaders International, Jonathan Worthington, Josh Bremerman, and John Soden. I appreciate each of you and the time you gave to reading and providing valuable feedback on the chapters.

I'm grateful to Carmen Imes for reading several of the Old Testament chapters and helping me think carefully about my "image of God" language. Thank you, Crystal Syring, for reading the completed manuscript and asking questions that helped me shore up some of the chapters in important ways. And thank you, Lori Galaske, for offering your professional editing skills near the end of the project, and for being an enthusiastic supporter of the book and the story it communicates.

To the series editor, Michael Morales, and to Rachel Hastings and her IVP Academic team, thank you for the invitation to write this volume, for your helpful feedback and encouragement, and for all the ways you have worked to see this book to fruition.

Finally, to Rebecca and Judah, thank you for reading every word of every chapter before the chapters were even good. I'm grateful for you both, and also for Elisha, Simeon, and Talia, for many prayers along the way and for your endurance through my highs and lows that for over a year largely revolved around how well or poorly the current chapter of the book was coming along. I love the five of you more than you can imagine.

APPENDIX A

QUESTIONS FOR REFLECTION AND DISCUSSION

INTRODUCTION: THE BEDROCK OF GLORY

1. When you think about glory—especially God's glory—what thoughts, ideas, or images come to mind? How would you define or describe God's glory to someone?

2. Have you ever thought about the relationship between God's pursuit of his glory and God's others-oriented love? Do these ideas seem compatible or incompatible to you? Does the way glory is defined in the introduction help resolve the seeming tension between these two things?

CHAPTER 1: GOD'S GLORY SHARED IN CREATION

3. Where in creation have you seen or experienced reflections of God? How have you seen God's glory in another human being? What effect did it have on you to encounter God's glory in creation or another person?

4. How does the vision of God's plan for his world and the part humans play in this plan help clarify your purpose or calling in the world?

What are some ways God has gifted or called you to express his glory and bring his goodness to your family, community, or workplace?

CHAPTER 2: GLORY LOST IN THE FALL

5. When we no longer trust God's graciousness and see his glory rightly (as happened in the Garden of Eden), it causes us to become takers rather than givers, self-protectors rather than outward-focused lovers. Where have you seen the effects of this in society? In your own life? How might beholding God's glory rightly free us from the need for self-seeking and self-protection and enable us to love, serve, and seek the good of others?

6. Think about the parts of the world you inhabit (your own life, your family, your community, your workplace, your country, etc.). Where do you see evidence of death, thorns and thistles, and life not fully flourishing under God's good rule and reign as he intended at creation? How does the picture of God's intention for his world presented so far help you to see this brokenness more clearly and envision something different and better for the world?

CHAPTER 3: GLORY TO AND THROUGH ISRAEL, PART ONE

7. God reveals his glory to Moses as both his gracious love and his justice and righteous judgment. Why is it necessary (and wonderful) that God's glory consist of both these aspects and not just one or the other? How is his commitment to merciful, forgiving love and also to justice good news for us and for the world?

8. The apostle Peter applies the identity and calling of Israel (treasured possession, kingdom of priests, holy nation) to Christians (see 1 Pet 2:9). What are some concrete or practical ways you, your family, or your church community might live as royal priests, representing God to the world and proclaiming the excellencies of him who called you out of darkness into his light?

CHAPTER 4: GLORY TO AND THROUGH ISRAEL, PART TWO

9. Have you ever thought of the law as being rooted in (and therefore revealing) the character and heart of God? How would it change the way you read and understand the laws in the Old Testament if you approached them asking the question, "What aspect of God's heart do I see in this command?"

10. Where do you see Adam and Israel's story in your own story? Have you ever "exchanged the glory of God for an image of an ox" (Ps 106:20)—substituting some lesser thing for God's glory that alone can satisfy? How does putting it in these terms help deepen a sense of the futility and evil of sin and draw your heart to repentance?

CHAPTER 5: ISAIAH: ALL FLESH WILL SEE THE GLORY OF THE LORD

11. Is there a particular idea, theme, or image from Isaiah's prophecies discussed in this chapter that you found encouraging, inspiring, or hopeful?

12. One of the ways Isaiah presents the coming of the Lord and the restoration of his kingship to the world is through imagery of creation personified: the desert rejoices with joy and singing and blossoms abundantly (Is 35:2), mountains and hills break forth into song, trees of the field clap their hands (Is 55:12). Why do you think Isaiah uses this imagery? What does it communicate about God's reign? What does it make you think or feel?

13. How does the emphasis of Isaiah (and of the whole Old Testament) on all flesh, all nations, all peoples seeing the glory of the Lord affect the way you think about the world and God's heart for people today?

CHAPTER 6: EZEKIEL: THE RETURN OF GLORY TO GOD'S TEMPLE

14. Ezekiel proclaims the truth that when we sin, we lie about God's character, "profan[ing] . . . his name . . . among the nations" (Ezek 36:21).

How have you seen Christians give God a bad reputation by their actions? How might you have done this?

15. On the other hand, how have you seen others reflect the truth about God through their lives in a way that is compelling or has helped you or others know more truly what God is like?

CHAPTER 7: THE GOSPEL OF JOHN: GLORY COMES DOWN

16. If, as John says, we see God's glory most fully in Jesus and know what God is like by looking at Jesus, what practical implications does this have for us as we seek to know God more? From looking at Jesus, what would you say God is like?

17. How have you experienced trust in response to beholding God's glory? What are some ways that knowing who God is has enabled you to trust and obey him in the face of fear, anxiety, trials, or temptation?

18. Does it seem significant to you that God's glory is most fully seen in Jesus' death on the cross? Why is this the case? What is it of God's glory we see in the cross? What might this mean about how we are to display God's glory in our own lives?

19. The Holy Spirit connects the glory of Jesus with the mission he gives his followers in the world. Reflect on the role of the Spirit in John's Gospel. What does he do? Why is he given to us? What does it make you think or feel to hear Jesus say that those who believe in him will have rivers of living water flowing from their hearts (Jn 7:38)? What might that look like in practical, everyday life?

CHAPTER 8: ROMANS: THE HOPE OF GLORY

20. When Paul indicts humanity for their response to God's glory in Romans 1, he says they did not glorify him as God or give thanks to him (Rom 1:21). Are you surprised that "not giving thanks" is included here? Why might ingratitude be such a big deal in Paul's mind? How has ingratitude led you to turn created things into substitutes for God's glory? Alternatively, think of moments of gratitude in your life. What

fruit has gratitude produced in you? What are some ways you might more intentionally practice gratitude?

21. How does the description of falling short of glory (Rom 3:23) in this chapter help you have a clearer sense of what it means to sin and also of what we were created for?

22. How have you seen God use trials and difficulties to develop his character in you (Rom 5:3) and conform you to the image of his Son (Rom 8:29)? How does this present work of the Spirit in you (transforming you, producing groanings in you, using "all things" as tools to accomplish God's good and loving designs in your life) encourage you and give hope?

CHAPTER 9: REVELATION: GLORY TO GOD AND TO THE LAMB FOREVER

23. What from John's picture of the end of the Bible's story in Revelation stands out to you? Why do you think this is?

24. How is the picture of a renewed creation in Revelation 21–22—of God dwelling with his people, his people reigning with Christ over his new creation, and glory filling the earth—different from other, popular ideas about eternal life? Are these differences significant? Why or why not?

CONCLUSION: BEHOLDING AND BECOMING

25. Where or in what ways have you beheld God's glory in your life?

26. What are some aspects of God's glory you have seen or experienced, and what effect has this had on you? Can you attest from your own experience to the way truly beholding his glory transforms us to be more like him?

APPENDIX B

"THE GLORY OF GOD" DEFINED BY VARIOUS THEOLOGIANS

Thomas Aquinas: "Therefore, knowledge of God's goodness is called glory in a most excellent sense, i.e., clear knowledge of the divine goodness accompanied by praise."[1]

John Owen: "The glory of God comprehends both the holy properties of his nature and the counsels of his will; and 'the light of the knowledge' of these things we have only 'in the face' or person 'of Jesus Christ.'"[2]

Jonathan Edwards: "The glory of God . . . is the emanation and true external expression of God's internal glory and fullness."[3]

Herman Bavinck: "The 'glory of the Lord' is the splendor and brilliance that is inseparably associated with all of God's attributes and his self-revelation

[1]Thomas Aquinas, *Commentary on the Letter of Saint Paul to the Hebrews*, on Heb 1:3, originally written in the thirteenth century, trans. Fabian R. Larche, ed. J. Mortensen and Enrique Alarcón (Lander, WY: Aquinas Institute for the Study of Sacred Doctrine, 2012), 15.

[2]John Owen, *Meditations and Discourses Concerning the Glory of Christ*, originally published in 1684 (London: Printed by J. A. for William Marshall, 1691), 14, https://quod.lib.umich.edu/e/eebo/A53707.0001.001/1:3.1.

[3]Jonathan Edwards, *The End for Which God Created the World*, originally published in 1765, in John Piper, *God's Passion for His Glory: Living the Vision of Jonathan Edwards with the Complete Text of "The End for Which God Created the World"* (Wheaton, IL: Crossway, 1998), 242.

in nature and grace, the glorious form in which he everywhere appears to his creatures."[4]

Karl Barth: "[God's glory] is the self-revealing sum of all divine perfections. It is the fullness of God's deity, the emerging, self-expressing and self-manifesting reality of all that God is."[5]

Hans Urs von Balthasar: "In the Old Testament this glory is the presence of Jahweh's lofty majesty in his covenant (and, mediated by the covenant, the presence of this majesty in the whole world). In the New Testament this glory shows itself as the love of God in Christ which descends 'to the end' (John 13:1) of death and night."[6]

J. I. Packer: Glory is "fundamental to God" and refers to his "excellence and praiseworthiness set forth in display."[7]

John Paul II: God's glory is the irradiation of his inner mystery.[8]

John Webster: "God's glory is God himself in the perfect majesty and beauty of his being. This glory is resplendent. . . . The enactment and form of this divine radiance is God the Son: he is the particular luminous reality in and as which the glory of God presents itself in its brightness."[9]

John Piper: "The term 'glory of God' in the Bible generally refers to the visible splendor or moral beauty of God's manifold perfections. . . . It is an attempt to put into words what cannot be contained in words—what God is like in his unveiled magnificence and excellence."[10]

Christopher Morgan: "The glory of God is the magnificence, worth, loveliness, and grandeur of his many perfections, which he displays in his

[4]Herman Bavinck, *Reformed Dogmatics,* vol. 2, *God and Creation,* originally published 1895–1899 (Grand Rapids, MI: Baker Academic, 2004), 252.

[5]Karl Barth, *Church Dogmatics,* originally published in 1957, ed. G. W. Bromiley and T. F. Torrance (New York: T&T Clark, 2004), 2.1:643.

[6]Hans Urs von Balthasar, *Glaubhaft ist nur Liebe,* 4th ed. (Einsiedeln: Johannes Verlag, 1975), 5-6.

[7]J. I. Packer, "The Glory of God," in *New Dictionary of Theology,* ed. Sinclair. B. Ferguson and David F. Wright (Downers Grove, IL: InterVarsity Press, 1998), 271-72.

[8]John Paul II, in Christopher West, *Word Made Flesh: A Companion to the Sunday Readings—Cycle C* (Notre Dame, IN: Ave Maria, 2018).

[9]John Webster, *God Without Measure: Working Papers in Christian Theology,* vol. 1, *God and the Works of God* (London: Bloomsbury T&T Clark, 2015), 73.

[10]John Piper, *Desiring God,* 2nd ed. (Portland, OR: Multnomah, 1986), 227.

creative and redemptive acts in order to make his glory known to those in his presence."[11]

Stephen Nichols: "Glory then becomes a sort of theological shorthand to encompass and communicate all that [God] is."[12]

C. John Collins: Glory becomes "a technical term for God's manifest presence."[13]

Sverre Aalen: God's manifestation of his person, presence, and/or works, especially his power, judgment, and salvation.[14]

Walter C. Kaiser Jr.: "Glory, then, is a special term that depicts God's visible and active presence."[15]

[11]Christopher Morgan, "The Glory of God," The Gospel Coalition, www.thegospelcoalition.org /essay/the-glory-of-god/.

[12]Stephen Nichols, "The Glory of God Present and Past," in *The Glory of God*, ed. Christopher Morgan (Wheaton, IL: Crossway, 2010), 29.

[13]C. John Collins, "*kabod*," in *New International Dictionary of Old Testament Theology and Exegesis*, ed. Willem A. VanGemeren (Grand Rapids, MI: Zondervan, 1997), 2:581-82.

[14]Sverre Aalen, "*doxa*," in *New International Dictionary of New Testament Theology*, ed. Colin Brown (Grand Rapids, MI: Zondervan, 1975–1978), 2:44-48.

[15]Walter C. Kaiser Jr., *The Majesty of God in the Old Testament: A Guide for Preaching and Teaching* (Grand Rapids, MI: Baker Academic, 2007), 120.

SCRIPTURE INDEX

ALSO IN THE ESBT SERIES

Exodus Old and New
978-0-8308-5539-1

Rebels and Exiles
978-0-8308-5541-4

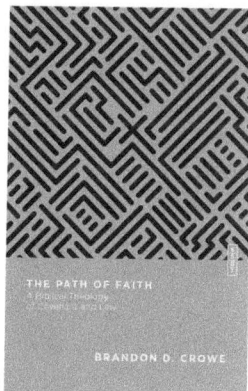

The Path of Faith
978-0-8308-5537-7

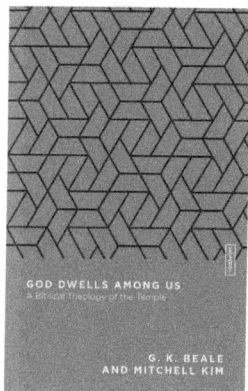

God Dwells Among Us
978-0-8308-5535-3

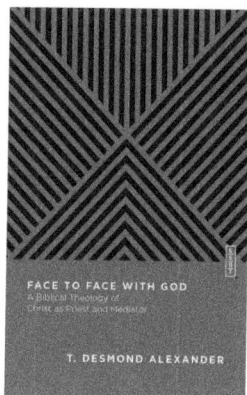

Face to Face with God
978-0-8308-4295-7

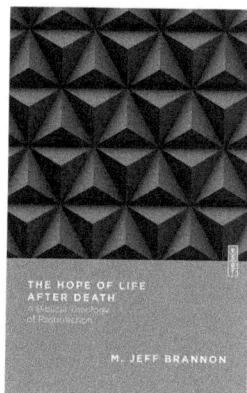

The Hope of Life After Death
978-0-8308-5531-5